Four Weeks to a
BETTER-BEHAVED
CHILD

Breakthrough Discipline
Techniques that Really Work

Cristine Chandler, Ph.D.,
WITH Laura McGrath

McGraw·Hill

New York   Chicago   San Francisco   Lisbon   London   Madrid   Mexico City
Milan   New Delhi   San Juan   Seoul   Singapore   Sydney   Toronto

The *McGraw·Hill* Companies

Library of Congress Cataloging-in-Publication Data

Chandler, Cristine.
 Four weeks to a better-behaved child : breakthrough discipline techniques that really work / by Cristine Chandler ; with Laura McGrath.—1st ed.
   p. cm.
 ISBN 0-07-143575-1 (alk. paper)
  1. Parenting—Handbooks, manuals, etc. 2. Child rearing—Handbooks, manuals, etc. I. McGrath, Laura. II. Title.

HQ772.C412 2004
649'.1—dc22   2003018018

1 2 3 4 5 6 7 8 9 0 AGM/AGM 3 2 1 0 9 8 7 6 5 4

ISBN 0-07-143575-1

McGraw-Hill books are available at special quantity discounts to use as premiums and sales promotions, or for use in corporate training programs. For more information, please write to the Director of Special Sales, Professional Publishing, McGraw-Hill, Two Penn Plaza, New York, NY 10121-2298. Or contact your local bookstore.

This book is printed on acid-free paper.

To my wonderful James

*From helping me design my dissertation
on paper napkins twenty-eight years ago to cheering
me on through each stage of this book—with love
and respect, you always encourage me to expect the
best from myself.*

Contents

Foreword

As a pediatrician of many years, I was often frustrated when I couldn't help parents deal with their children's behavior problems. I find this book immensely valuable, and so will parents and other caregivers. This book provides step-by-step guidelines for managing and preventing many behavior problems. It points out that anger and punishment are the least effective means to achieve better behavior. The 4 Cs—consistent use of clear, contingent consequences, and the power of parents' attention and inattention are the foundations of successful child rearing. The new techniques of "No Reply" and "Cool Down" are described in practical ways for parents to follow.

Whereas *Dr. Spock's Baby and Child Care* was the seminal parenting book for a previous generation, Dr. Chandler's *Four Weeks to a Better Behaved Child* will become the parenting "bible" for today's parents and the professionals who help them. I don't make this comparison lightly. Dr. Benjamin Spock provided parents with a much-needed commonsense guide based on his clinical experience. One of his greatest contributions was to give parents greater confidence in their own abilities to care for their children.

Dr. Chandler's book comes at a very different time in history, but at a time when guidance for parents is once again sorely needed. In many households, there is only one parent or both parents work. Television and outside activities (some good, some not) absorb much of children's time and attention. Parents have little time with their children, and many are reluctant to use this time setting limits and sticking to them. As a result, many children are growing up without the discipline they need to be successful in life. Today's parents also share child rearing with child care centers, nannies, babysitters, and others, making child rearing a "village" responsibility. Dr. Chandler's book will help parents navigate these and other challenges.

Dr. Chandler not only draws on extensive clinical experience, as Dr. Spock did, but her book is also firmly grounded in the fifty years of child development research that has been conducted since his book first appeared. Since Dr. Spock reacted against the overly strict child rearing of the 1920s and 1930s, his book was sometimes misinterpreted as promoting permissive parenting. Dr. Chandler's book, on the other hand, is very clear and specific, and it describes highly effective, proven techniques. It offers parents a loving but firm approach to discipline, which they can use to teach their children how to manage their own behavior. The result will be children who grow into confident, productive citizens.

Generations of parents and children will benefit from this important guide.

—Robert J. Haggerty, MD

Dr. Haggerty is Professor and Chair Emeritus of Pediatrics at the University of Rochester School of Medicine and Dentistry. From 1980 to 1992, he was president of the William T. Grant Foundation, whose main focus is to support education and research on behavioral pediatrics. In 1984 and '85, he served as president of the American Academy of Pediatrics, an organization with a current membership of more than 55,000 American pediatricians. He was the first to use the term "the new morbidities" to describe the change in pediatrics from a profession primarily dealing with physical disease to one dealing more and more with problems of development and behavior among children.

Acknowledgments

My wish to write a helpful book for parents about child discipline techniques has come to fruition after a thirty-year journey. Many great teachers, supporters, friends, and family members have provided invaluable help in understanding children and parents, and how they can best live happily together.

The scholars and clinicians in my academic family tree provided the learning and guidance I needed to become a psychologist. Thanks to Fred Grote at Western Washington University for introducing me to developmental psychology and starting me on this extraordinarily rewarding career. My University of Denver professors added their invaluable expertise in developmental psychology. To Marshall Haith, Joe Campos, Kurt Fischer, and Brian McWhinney, thank you for your intellect and wisdom. A special thanks to my dissertation adviser and friend, Susan Harter, who guided me in my pursuit of understanding children's motivation. Also, I could not have become the clinician I am today without the astute teaching and guidance of Paula Bernstein. Finally, my deep gratitude to Gorden Ulrey, who taught me how to see and understand each child as a unique individual, and to bring patience and humor to my daily work.

I also want to acknowledge the contribution of Laura McGrath, my dedicated and hardworking writer. Through listening and questioning, she helped me translate my ideas and experiences into this practical volume for parents. And we had fun doing it, which is the greatest compliment of all!

Last, to all the parents, children, and families who have allowed me to enter their lives, I extend my deep gratitude. Through you, I learned about the multiple varied ways that families love, support, and nurture one another—and, yes, sometimes hurt each other just trying to get through the day. Thank you for letting me help you find more peaceful ways of being a family. This book is dedicated to your ongoing success in raising well-adjusted children who know how to expect and deliver the best in themselves.

Dear Parents . . .

. . . and grandparents, teachers, and others who care about the youngsters in their charge, Do your children sometimes act up? Do they sometimes stomp off mad, slam the door, shout, defy you, or do things you've repeatedly told them not to do? Conversely, do they sometimes ignore you, dawdle, or fail to do the things you've asked them to do?

Do you sometimes find yourself getting angry? Do you get tired of repeating yourself? Do you raise your voice, shout, scream, even feel like throwing things sometimes? Have you tried various discipline techniques but had no consistent, long-term success?

If you said no to all of these questions, then put this book down—you don't need it. Moreover, you're probably superhuman! Because all the preceding scenarios are absolutely normal for most children and parents.

Having said that, I want to tell you that such behaviors—yours or your children's—do not have to be a way of life. If you believe your children misbehave too often, or you find yourself frustrated and angry too often, then this book is written especially for you. Its subject is child discipline—discipline that *works*.

My biggest goal is to help parents raise their children in ways that help them become happy, productive individuals. This book is designed to help you achieve that. In the following chapters, I explain a fairly simple system of behavioral regulation—or discipline—that works for children between the ages of two and twelve. It works at home and away from home. It works when kids are wired and when they are tired. It works for those who master concepts instantly and those who struggle to learn. It works for the wordy and the withdrawn, the sunny and the sullen.

The introduction that follows tells you a little about my background and about what you'll find in this book. Be assured that the system I describe in this book is built on a solid foundation of widely accepted theory and derived from a wealth of experience with parents and kids. I wrote this book with the deepest respect for you, and with the most profound empathy for the steadfast daily dedication and wisdom that it takes to raise a child.

With my very best wishes,
CRISTINE CHANDLER, PH.D.

Introduction

Parents want—more than almost anything on earth—to raise good kids who grow into happy, well-adjusted, responsible adults. Sometimes, however, this turns out to be more difficult than most of us imagined.

For the past twenty-five years, I have been working with parents and children in my clinical psychology practice. Most of the time, parents call me because their kids are "driving them crazy!" Almost always, the underlying issue turns out to be the big "D"—discipline—and the problems range from mild to severe. Regardless of the severity, I can help about 95 *percent* of these parents solve their discipline problems. They are astonished and grateful to find that they make enormous progress in just *two weeks*. Within a month, the discipline problems are largely solved—and *stay solved*.

Just in case you're thinking, "Oh, but our situation is different," let me share just three examples of discipline issues I've worked with.

Example 1: Bill and Cathy were very concerned because the only discipline technique that seemed to work with Kyle was to get very angry. "Kyle doesn't obey us unless we scream at him," they said. In two sessions, I taught them my techniques, and within those two weeks, they began to practice them. Immediately, the angry interchanges stopped, and Kyle's behavior improved remarkably. Their household became more peaceful—and stayed that way.

Example 2: Joyce and Henry had been using Time-Out and decided it just didn't work. Jessie would not go to Time-Out, or if she did, she would not stay there—hence, her behavior did not change. I taught them my Cool Down technique and explained how it differed from the Time-Out technique they had been practicing. As always, I gave them very specific directions. That same night, they explained to Jessie how Cool Down would work. Then they put it into practice the very next time she acted out. After the third time they used Cool Down, Jessie started to comply with their directions without getting angry. As a result, she soon took more control over her own actions and became a much better-behaved—and happier—child.

Example 3: Suzanne, a busy single mom, was caught up in what she rightly considered to be a system of bribes to get nine-year-old Colin to do his chores. She and Colin seemed to be constantly haggling, with his demands for rewards steadily increasing or changing. After learning how consequences can be used to influence behavior and how to apply my Learned Rewards system, she restructured the chores and the reward system. Now Colin's incentive to earn his reward time is so strong that he does his tasks every day without arguing.

I could tell you thousands of stories—and this book includes a number of examples based on experiences of families in my practice. In fact, I've had such extraordinary success that my collection of stories grows daily. As word has grown of parents' success with my techniques, my phone has been ringing off the hook. Pediatricians refer their patients and tell their colleagues, who in turn refer their patients. Parents pass the word along to their friends and neighbors. Even many dads who were at first skeptical of seeing a psychologist have become vocal advocates because they appreciate the logic—and the success—of my approach. My calendar now overflows, and I have had to turn away clients. This is not a happy situation for me, since I entered the field of clinical psychology precisely because I want to help people solve their problems.

My dilemma has become, how can I help all these people and also reach out to others who want to do a better job of child discipline? One solution, strongly urged by pediatricians and parents alike: write a book!

So here it is, the essence of what I teach my clients.

What Does This Book Offer You?

Four Weeks to a Better-Behaved Child provides you with a practical system of discipline based on a positive premise: children behave well when they understand clearly what is expected of them and they are held accountable. The parents' job is to make their expectations very clear and then to apply an appropriate consequence every time their child complies—or fails to comply.

The book describes the underlying foundation for discipline in terms of the 4 Cs: clear, consistent, contingent consequences. It then outlines four specific discipline techniques that parents can use to put these 4 Cs into daily practice. Two of the techniques encourage children to turn desirable behaviors into regular habits; the other two discourage children from repeating unwanted ones. All four techniques are meticulously constructed on proven behavioral principles for managing behavior and on the knowledge of what children can understand and act on at any given age.

Thus, by reading *A Better-Behaved Child*, you will learn specific discipline techniques you can put into immediate use. Every bit as important, however, you will also learn *when* and *why* certain discipline techniques work (or fail to work). As a result, you will be able to analyze a situation and determine which discipline method to use in order to achieve a desired result. In addition, if you are like many parents, you will likely find yourself becoming more thoughtful about the ways you communicate with your children. You may be surprised to discover that simply making your expectations clearer goes a long way toward eliciting good behavior. By applying the approach and techniques outlined in this book, you can expect to see positive results within four weeks.

Why Does *This* Discipline System Work?

Why does this discipline system work for parents who have had only partial success or quite often, complete failure with other techniques? This system differs from the others in several important ways.

First, many parents tell me that some books on child discipline are so complicated that they just quit reading, while other books describe techniques that require many months of effort before any change in behavior occurs. So my system's first two differences are straightforward: this book is easy to read, and these techniques get results very quickly.

Second, the power of this system of discipline becomes very apparent as this book overturns some commonly held beliefs. One such belief concerns punishment. When asked to name the single most powerful discipline tool at their disposal, many parents identify punishment. In reality, however, this is often the least effective discipline technique, and this book explains why.

Another commonly held belief relates to anger. Anger surfaces regularly in many families, and sometimes it escalates very quickly. Most parents wind up feeling terrible when this happens, and they feel guilty and worried about the negative impact it may have on their children. At the same time, however, many parents have come to believe that sometimes anger is the only way they can get their children to behave. They say, "I don't want to get so angry, but it's the only thing that works." *A Better-Behaved Child* explains why—quite apart from making everyone feel bad—anger is totally ineffective as a means of lasting discipline.

The book also takes on the popular and widely used Time-Out technique. Many parents use this technique without having learned exactly how to apply it or what factors influence its success. Moreover, sometimes the teaching of this technique is flawed. Because easily made mistakes can cause Time-Out to be completely ineffective, many parents just give up on it. *A Better-Behaved Child* offers an alternative technique called Cool Down. While similar to Time-Out in many ways, it corrects that technique's potential flaws. The result: Cool Down is a highly effective discipline tool.

One final way this book differs from others—and one reason these techniques work—stems from my professional training and experience. My background differs from many others in the children's mental health profession in that I have done extensive work in two separate but related fields: *child development* and *clinical psychology*. In my training and clinical work, I've studied what motivates children to behave in various ways. I've also examined how various parenting techniques impact children's behavior. Early on, I found that the quickest and most successful way to change the behavior of a child is to change the behavior of the parent. Thus, throughout my years of clinical practice, I have worked with both children and their parents—thousands of them. The combined approach—understanding what motivates people to behave and what children can understand and act on at various stages of their development—underlies the system of behavioral regulation that I have developed and then refined through my years in clinical practice.

This book brings together the depth and breadth of learning I have acquired from my training, research, and clinical experience with families. The core discipline techniques presented here are refined, condensed, and very clearly written to make this discipline system easy to use.

One qualification: although I've had success using these techniques with children exhibiting serious emotional or mental problems (autism, bipolar, or other serious clinical disorders), this book will not address the additional issues these families face. While such families may find this book to be a useful tool in the context of a larger therapeutic program, it is not intended to be a standalone strategy for them.

Watch for These Important Themes

You will find some themes repeated throughout this book. The first is that the *single most powerful tool parents have at their disposal is the attention they give their children.* You will come to understand that giving and limiting your attention is the single most powerful discipline technique you can use.

The second theme is that *children behave best when their parents practice what I call the 4 Cs: clear, consistent use of contingent consequences.* I explain these in greater detail in Chapter 3. Simply put, the 4 Cs mean providing your children with very clear expectations for their behavior, and having them understand that they will experience positive or negative consequences contingent upon their behavior. Now the hard part—consistency. These clear expectations and contingent consequences must be practiced day in and day out, at home and away from home, whether you or your child is sick or well, glad or sad, wired or tired. Employing these 4 Cs will help reduce the frequency and intensity of anger, which occurs so easily but can undermine the relationships children have with their parents and the effectiveness of discipline as well.

How This Book Is Organized

If you are reading *A Better-Behaved Child*, then you probably think you need it! Things are not going as smoothly as you'd like them to with your children. Maybe you even feel that you are in a parenting crisis.

How you approach this book depends in part on you. Do you want to understand the whole context for the discipline techniques you may choose to undertake, or would you prefer to focus immediately on the *how-tos* rather than the *whys*? Of course, whether you start at the beginning or in the middle of this book depends on how urgently you need to change what's occurring right now in your household.

I recommend that you read the whole book straight through from start to finish; it will not take long. The first four chapters provide a foundation and framework for the how-tos presented in the last five chapters. Chapter 1 begins with a brief overview of why children need structure and discipline in their lives. Chapter 2 addresses the problem of anger—why it occurs and what impact it has. Chapter 3 focuses on the concept of consequences as the foundation for discipline, and explains if-then thinking, the 4 Cs, and the power inherent in parents' attention. These chapters are fairly short—as is, intentionally, the whole book—and they help you understand why the techniques work, and why they must be used exactly as they are explained.

If you really cannot wait to get right into the discipline techniques, then start with Chapter 4. This chapter describes positive reinforcement, negative reinforcement, extinction, and punishment—the four fundamental behavioral principles that form the basis for my discipline techniques. If you skip these, you may not fully understand what follows in the remaining chapters.

Chapter 5 lays out two techniques employing positive reinforcement. These tools can be used to encourage children to adopt the behaviors their parents desire. Chapter 6 answers some common questions about these techniques.

Chapter 7 presents two techniques for eliminating or decreasing unwanted behaviors. One of these is Cool Down, a relative of the widely used Time-Out technique but with some differences that enable its success. Chapter 8 deals with some of the nitty-gritty questions about Cool Down—what happens if . . . ? Exceptional circumstances always occur, so this chapter helps you find creative, effective ways to apply Cool Down even when it is not obvious how to do so.

Chapter 9 puts the whole system together and addresses what happens as the system begins to work, as the kids change, and as life changes. The Appendix at the end of the book is a table that outlines children's capabilities at each developmental stage and how those capabilities relate to discipline.

Now if I were you, I would be at least a little bit skeptical. Every day, we're promised "miracles" in the advertising of everything from cars to medicine to the "perfect" vacation. Certainly, I do not want to suggest that this book will automatically solve all your discipline problems. No book can, and no set of techniques can without you actively using your brain, experience, values, personality, and above all, consistent application of the same clear contingent consequences. Having said that, I feel confident that the techniques described in this book can help you to help your child become better behaved in just four weeks. After all, you already care very deeply, and very soon, you'll have knowledge of proven techniques to turn your positive intentions into more effective parenting.

Now, to begin—read, use what you learn, and treasure the results!

Why Children Need Discipline

Emily pounded the floor, wailing and crying.
Between ragged breaths, she sobbed, "You're always
yelling at me. I'm always in trouble, but I don't
know why."

As children grow and develop, their needs change. They need increasing amounts of freedom to make decisions, ways to express their individuality, appropriate places to make messes, new kinds of reassurance, and at times, astonishing quantities of food!

One fundamental principle, however, does not change: throughout their growing-up years, *children need consistent structure. This enables them to feel secure and behave appropriately.* When routines are established for eating meals, going to bed, finishing homework, and doing chores, the children know what to expect and they respond accordingly—most of the time. Likewise, when consistent expectations are set regarding how they must behave and interact with others, children feel more comfortable and are more likely to act appropriately. Conversely, children who experience inconsistent expectations simply do not know how to behave their best. As a result, they try out a variety of behaviors, including undesirable ones.

Having the same rules—and the same consequences—in place all the time gives a child a great sense of security. These give order to his world; they show him his place in it.

In addition to a certain sense of security, another important positive effect results from providing children with clear standards of behavior: social acceptance. Although parents tend to focus on their own children's sweetness and to excuse their misdeeds, other people do not see misbehaving children through the same soft-hued lenses. Thus, children who are allowed to misbehave experience negative reactions from others around them. For young children, the consequences may not be too substantial. But as youngsters grow to school age, friends, teachers, and others expect them to behave in socially acceptable ways. When they do not, they may be ostracized by their peers and get in trouble with teachers and others in charge.

When these children are allowed to continue such habits unchecked, they can have more serious difficulty later on with authority figures, and frequently act out—sometimes in destructive or self-destructive ways. Misbehaving children who are bullied by their peers, scolded by their teachers, or chastised by other adults miss having the reaffirming social experiences that add to their sense of security and well-being, and that help them grow into successful, contented adults.

The Need for Consistency

Especially when they become old enough to understand the concept of rules, children both want and need clear expectations and rules for their behavior. They also want these to be the same for other members of their family. Although children sometimes cannot manage or "regulate" their behavior to meet all of these rules and expectations, they find it comforting to have a standard of behavior set for them. Children want, more than anything else, to please their parents; therefore, they usually strive to behave in ways that are expected of them, if these are made clear.

Even if they do not abide by all the rules, all the time, children find it comforting to know both what is expected of them and that those expectations remain the same, day after day.

Creating and applying rules consistently is, of course, far easier said than done. Many families can establish a reasonably regular household schedule and routine, although this may be harder when both parents hold jobs and sometimes are required to travel or meet other responsibilities as well. What many parents find far more difficult, however, is to apply discipline consistently. One common symptom of the breakdown in consistency is when parents make excuses for their child's misbehavior. They may say she was naughty because she was tired, or hungry, or overstimulated, or bored, or ate sugar, or is going through a phase, or . . . ! But what children really want and need is to have the same rules apply under all those circumstances and others besides. Parents must decide on the most appropriate response to their child's misbehavior in context of the circumstances that influence it. The child needs to learn, however, that the standards of behavior are not adjusted on a whim. She needs to learn that she is expected to behave according to established rules even when she is tired, hungry, overstimulated, or bored.

EMILY, THE FIVE-year-old whose sobs began this chapter, reflects outwardly every child's deep internal need to understand what is expected of her all the time.

Just before her outburst, Emily had been scolded for taking her peanut butter and jelly sandwich into the living room. The day before, her mother had allowed Emily to eat a turkey sandwich in front of the TV—in that very same living room.

From Mom's perspective, she snapped at Emily this time because she envisioned the inevitable grape jelly stains on the white carpet, whereas yesterday's turkey would not have left a spot. From Emily's point of view, however, the rules had changed. Like all five-year-olds, she wanted to please her mother. So when she was scolded for doing something she thought was "right," she reacted with hurt and frustration— all exaggerated because she was not quite old enough to control her emotions. What Emily needed was for Mom to explain the rule clearly and then apply it in the same way every day.

Of course, the child needs to see her parents likewise hold themselves accountable to the same standards under varying circumstances. Will parents behave consistently all the time? Of course not. Parents experience stress, too. They get tired, hungry, overstimulated, bored, and maybe even go through phases! Moreover, they must deal with other significant pressures compounding their stress. They must pay the bills, get the furnace fixed, wash the clothes, manage a household and their jobs, and worry over their children's, their parents', or their own illnesses—the list is endless. So, of course, parents will not establish and maintain perfect, consistent compliance with rules for their children or themselves. But to the extent that they can, they provide their children with one of life's most important foundations—a sense of security, and a pattern of if-then thinking that will enable the children to regulate their own behavior throughout their lives.

Within a consistent framework, wise parents "grow" their family's rules and consequences to accommodate their children's growth and development and the changing circumstances of their lives.

Most parents find it challenging to develop and maintain rules and expectations that are appropriate to each child in the family as well as to the various circumstances that influence the whole family every day. Their job becomes even more challenging because, of course, neither children nor the parents themselves are frozen in time. Children grow, circumstances change, and the rules must change with them. Among other things, rules must allow for the growth of children's cognitive abilities. Children need to learn the relationship between their behavior and consequences, and they can develop this understanding only when the rules grow along with them.

For example, a city-dwelling parent may make an inflexible rule for a two-year-old: he must never go into the street without holding Mom or Dad's hand. After he turns four, Mom and Dad change the rule to recognize his growing ability: he no longer has to hold hands, but he must never go in the street without Mom or Dad. The rule for the six-year-old prepares him for future independence: Mom or Dad still must accompany him, but now he is required to look both ways to watch for oncoming cars. At age eight, he may be allowed to cross the street after looking both ways—as long as Mom or Dad is watching. When he is ten, the child may be allowed to cross certain streets after telling Mom or Dad where he is going, but other roads may still be too dangerous for him to cross alone. In each case, the rule is based on the child's ability to understand and apply it. The two-year-old cannot control his own behavior, so the rule is simple and absolute, whereas the ten-year-old is skilled at reasoning and can apply a rule that allows him to use his own judgment.

The rules are also influenced by many other factors—other children in the family; other caregivers who administer the rules; moving to a different neighborhood; friends, neighbors, and schools with different rules; and other aspects of daily life. Given the multiple, and sometimes conflicting, factors that affect discipline, it is no surprise that parents find it difficult to apply appropriate rules consistently. The sands constantly shift under their feet. As their children grow, the transitions in ability and readiness are not always clear. Extenuating circumstances occur—and often at the worst possible times. So the parents' job is not entirely clear-cut and certainly not easy. Nonetheless, if parents can hold to the big picture and maintain consistency as best as they possibly can, they will do well by their children.

If Children Want Discipline, Why Do They Test Limits?

As deeply as children desire to please their parents, they also want to satisfy their own impulses. The child's desire for self-gratification, more than almost anything else, conflicts with parents' needs in the early years. The preschooler feels like dawdling through breakfast, but Mom needs to get the child out the door so she can go to work. The kindergartner playing tag with his friends does not want to stop, but now it is bedtime. The seven-year-old is engrossed in a computer game, but she has only an hour left in which to finish her untouched homework. In each of these very normal circumstances lies the potential for battle.

C hildren test rules because deep down they want to find the limits.

Are these children unusually defiant? No, they are just being kids. Sometimes kids test the boundaries just to see what they are. If kids learn frequently and consistently that the rules are always the same, their need to test them diminishes.

Parents often tell me that their children behave quite well at school but are holy terrors at home. In almost every circumstance, when a child behaves well in one place and badly in another, the problem is not with the child but with the responsible adults.

Psychologists describe this phenomenon as a "performance deficit," as opposed to an "ability deficit." A child with an ability deficit cannot perform a particular behavior in any environment. The solution is to fix the problem with the child, which usually means teaching her how to perform a task or adopt a certain behavior. A child with a performance deficit can perform a behavior in one setting but not in another. In this case, the problem is not with the child but with the environment. Creating a consistent structure for the child often resolves this situation. Once she understands that the same rules and expectations will be applied all the time, she will soon alter her performance to correspond with the environment as she perceives it.

MR. AND MRS. M. came to me distraught. Their seven-year-old son's teacher reported that Richard was a model child in school—polite, considerate, and attentive. At home, however, he had tantrums so violent that he threw objects and broke toys.

What soon became evident was that while the school environment provided a clear, consistent set of rules and expectations, the home environment did not. Even though the parents had the best of intentions, they had not established a set of standards for Richard's behavior, and they reacted to his rages with a progression of predictable but conflicting signals. When he whimpered, they cajoled. As his anger mounted, they told him they would ignore him—but they did not. They reasoned, then pleaded, then shouted, then threatened, and finally became physical. "We don't want to spank him," they said, "but he gives us no choice."

What Richard sorely needed was not a spanking, but a home environment where the standards were as clear and consistent as the school's.

For some parents, the discipline problem stems from a real fear of setting limits. In the early twentieth century, Sigmund Freud introduced the notion that harsh treatment in early childhood could damage children's personalities. His theory has been interpreted, reinterpreted, and misinterpreted over the past century. Thus today, quasi-Freudian mythology still colors the thinking of some parents, and they mistakenly believe that "discipline" equals "damage." Additionally, with the prevalent discussions of child abuse in schools and on television, some parents worry that their children will find them emotionally, if not physically, abusive. Although such concerns are understandable, parents need to recognize the very real difference between abuse and firm, consistent discipline that is administered lovingly and fairly.

Still other parents may believe they are setting limits for their children, even the same kinds of limits that their own parents had set for them as children. In actuality, when they examine the specifics of their behavior, they discover that they are not setting limits but are reacting to the particulars of the moment. Without a consistent set of standards, these parents say "yes" because they cannot find an immediate reason to say "no," or they automatically say "no" but then change to "yes" when the child wheedles. They confuse reacting to the moment with clearly setting and maintaining standards and rules. Given such a confusing environment, what typical child would set his own limits or control his own impulses?

While children go through the natural stages of development, with all of the attendant changes in abilities, parents must help them learn to become strong, rational adults who make wise decisions and choices about their lives. That is a tall order for anyone. But through discipline designed with forethought and applied with consistency—as well as with love, of course—parents can succeed.

2

Anger: A Pitfall Even for Conscientious Parents

I just don't understand why I get so furious when this little bitty kid starts screaming in the grocery store. After all, I'm supposed to be the grown-up!

Oh my! This frustration is so real—and so common. Most parents are kind, conscientious people. They treat others with respect and consideration. They fully intend to treat their children the same way. BK (Before Kids), they could handle their emotions and their lives with composure. They managed jobs and households, and they dealt with coworkers, neighbors, vendors, and a host of people and situations on a daily basis, all with calm and dignity. So when they now find themselves suddenly swept up in anger—provoked, no less, by a person one-fifth their size and over whom they are "supposed" to have control—they are both astonished and upset.

Anger is one of the most common pitfalls of parenting. It is important for parents to recognize and deal with their anger, because almost without fail, it has very negative outcomes. *The most serious negative outcome of anger is that it undermines a most criti-*

How often do we all witness the following scenario? In a grocery store aisle, a child whines, begging for a treat. The parent refuses. The child becomes louder and more insistent. The parent responds angrily. After a few rounds in this unlikely ring, the whole situation has escalated, and both child and parent are hollering at full volume. Then the parent shouts: "Now you just stop that yelling. I want you to calm down—right now!"

A good idea, most observers would agree, but how can this child be expected to control his emotions when the parent is shouting at him?

cal lesson that parents must teach their children: how to manage their own emotions. One fundamental behavioral pattern that differentiates adults from children is the ability to regulate emotions internally. We expect adults to be able to cope calmly and logically with a wide range of situations, including some that certainly might justify an angry response. Adults are expected to deal with disappointments, conflicts, contradictions, pressures, unfair judgments, and many other negative situations with complete composure— that is, without "losing their cool." A very occasional outburst is usually excused, but when adults repeatedly fail to manage their own emotions—even for what might seem to be a just cause— they are labeled as "immature." In other words, they are characterized as childlike.

In order to help their children develop the mature behavior that will be expected of them, parents must teach them how to handle a variety of situations with their emotions under control. Thus most parents patiently teach their children how to deal with a bully on the school playground, cope with an unkind remark by an insensitive adult, do chores they dislike without complaint—all with self-control. As their children grow older and encounter more sophisticated problems, parents help them learn how to work these out by using logic—analyzing alternatives and rationally selecting the most appropriate solution.

Learning how to manage emotions is one of the most important lessons that parents undertake to teach. But it is seriously undermined if the interchanges between parent and child are routinely marked by anger.

Nearly all child psychologists agree that anger is a negative force in parenting. But few, if any, explain what impact anger has in the total scheme of effective discipline. This chapter provides some information about why anger occurs, how it impacts both parents and children, and why it is unsuccessful and even damaging as a discipline technique. As I have worked with parents, most have found that once they understood these "whys" and "hows," they were far more able to control their own anger and largely eliminate it from their repertoire of parenting techniques.

Why Anger Occurs

Most of the parents I see in my practice experience enormous frustration over the spiral that occurs when they begin by quietly giving an instruction but end up shouting. They repeat an instruction over and over without getting their child to comply, and finally, they become angry. Sometimes they just lose control; at other times, they deliberately choose to show anger because they believe it is the only way they can get through to the child and make her understand that they are serious. In some cases, their anger becomes so intense that their own ferocity frightens them.

When an expectation is unmet or contradicted, both children and adults may respond with anger. Sometimes families establish patterns of behavior in which children routinely defy expectations and parents routinely respond with anger. No one wins in these situations, and no one is happy with them.

Everybody gets angry, at one time or another. It is a response people seem to be born with. During childhood, parents help children learn how to reprogram that part of their wiring. By the time most people reach adulthood, they are well able to manage that particular emotion, with only occasional exceptions.

Generally, anger is caused by an unmet or contradicted expectation. We expect something to happen but it does not, or the opposite occurs, and sometimes we respond with anger.

Infants become angry because they do not get their way—the most fundamental version of having unmet expectations. They get hungry, and when they are not fed, they react with anger. They get tired, and when their need for rest is not immediately met, they get cranky or sometimes downright furious. Without having access to words, they express themselves in the only way they can: by screaming, crying, holding their breath, or flailing their hands and feet.

As babies grow, they express their anger in ways that reflect their increasing control over their motor and verbal skills, if not yet their emotions. They use words to communicate their anger, and they lash out with their fists or feet with more deliberate effect. Young children often anger quickly—a carryover from preverbal stages when they had no options but to act out their feelings. Now, however, they not only cry but also shout, scream, and throw objects. If children are not taught early in life how to manage their anger, they may carry these patterns forward into adulthood.

School-age children who are learning how to manage their emotions still may react with anger under certain conditions. The most common of these conditions are tiredness and hunger—two fundamental needs that may trigger reactions associated with the same situations in infancy. For the most part, however, youngsters at this age are learning that angry behavior such as screaming, hitting, stomping, or kicking will produce unwanted outcomes— unless, of course, these behaviors become part of a routine scenario with Mom and Dad. Here is where the problems occur: when anger meets anger.

Why do parents get angry? Generally, parents anger more quickly with their own children than with other children or adults, because the emotional stakes are higher. Parents care more deeply about their own children's behavior because they have more invested in the outcome, which is nothing short of their offspring's success as human beings.

Parents expect their children to behave in certain ways. Unaccustomed to being defied in other aspects of their lives, parents become upset when their progeny fail to follow their directions or flat-out contradict them. When children violate parents' expectations, a spiral of responses often occurs.

In these situations, parents seldom begin by showing anger. They may repeat the rule or the expectation, or they may patiently and calmly explain why the child must perform in a certain way. "When you throw your toy, it could break the TV. Then you would not have a TV to watch." "Don't take your sister's toy without asking. It does not belong to you. You don't want her to take your toys away from you, so you must not take hers from her, either. That's part of how we share." "When you pull the dog's

NINE-YEAR-OLD Kari has honed "Just a minute" to a fine art. She routinely stretches out her computer games longer and longer, successfully stalling the moment of shutdown during her parent's countless repetitions of "It's time now," and "Kari, you have to stop."

So when does she turn off the computer? "I stop playing when Dad comes to the top of the stairs. When he gets there, I know he's mad and I'd better do what he says." Translation: everything her parents say up to that point is just noise! Discipline is not really enforced until Dad gets angry.

tail, it hurts him. He gets a boo-boo, just like you do sometimes. You don't want him to feel bad, do you?"

Very often, however, patient explanations fail to get the desired effect, so the parents raise the intensity up a notch. They speak more firmly and sometimes issue ultimatums. "I told you not to throw your toy. I mean it. Don't do that anymore." "If you throw your toy again, I will take it away from you." Or even, "If you throw that toy one more time, I will take it away and you will never get it back."

Finally, when this more serious level of demand is not met and the child is still noncompliant, parents' emotions become engaged and they get angry. Then they make threats they cannot possibly keep: "If you do that one more time, you will never watch TV again!" They shout, scream, or even become physical—shaking, yanking, or smacking their child. Inevitably, in calmer moments they deeply regret such outbursts.

For both children and parents, an angry interchange is often a learned behavior that becomes more deeply ingrained with each repetition. They practice the same scenario over and over again: the child misbehaves, the parent corrects him, the child continues, the parent becomes more and more firm, the child continues, and finally, the parent explodes. In times of stress, the triggers for such episodes are even more immediate and such scenarios more frequent. No one is happy with this pattern. And . . . it does not work.

The Impact of Anger

Apart from making everyone unhappy, anger produces several very negative outcomes. This section outlines *four negative outcomes* that have a significant impact on parents' ability to discipline their children effectively.

THE EFFECTS OF ANGER

1. Anger begets anger.
2. Anger impairs the ability to process information and think logically.
3. Parents' anger gives attention to children for misbehaving.
4. Anger makes parents feel bad.

---

1. The first and most obvious effect of parents' angry outbursts is the one every psychologist points out: *angry parents model a behavior they do not want their children to adopt.* When a child witnesses his parents shout at or strike one another, or when he becomes the target of such displays of anger, he is learning by example. With such teaching, he is likely to adopt these behaviors. No matter how frequently children are told not to be angry, nothing outweighs *showing* them how to manage conflict without anger.

2. A slightly less obvious outcome of anger is one that seldom, if ever, appears in print: *anger impairs the ability to process information and to think logically*. Nearly every adult understands this principle in the context of an argument with a spouse or partner. Words spoken in the heat of the moment bear little resemblance to those used when addressing a situation calmly. On the other side of a shouting match, a person who is the target of an insult often cannot come back with a reasonable response. Under normal circumstances, that same individual could very well counter a criticism with a logical response. In the heat of the moment, however, he cannot think how to respond. Research has, in fact, demonstrated that anger impairs the ability to think clearly.

Thus, when a parent becomes emotionally engaged, he cannot communicate effectively or teach his child what he wants her to

JAN, AN INTELLIGENT young mother, came to me distraught by the increasing frequency and intensity of her anger at her son. When I asked her to describe a typical situation, she told me the following incident:

"He deliberately disobeyed me for the third time in a row, and I snapped. I found myself not only telling him what he had done wrong, but shouting at him that he was stupid and lazy, and furthermore, that he drooled into his pillow at night, and that he was getting fat because he ate too much. None of this had anything to do with his disobeying me, and I was really horrified that I said these terrible things to him and hurt his feelings needlessly."

What happened to Jan often happens with anger: angry people actually lose the ability to think logically or act rationally.

learn. When angry, he is more likely to say things that are confusing at best and harmful at worst. So the stakes for learning to discipline children without anger are high.

The impact of children's anger is even greater. Angry children are even less able than angry adults to process information. They can neither understand nor put to use any of the explanations that even the calmest of parents provide at these times. From such interactions, angry children discover instead that their misbehavior earns them their parents' attention.

Not only does getting angry impair a child's ability to think logically—an emerging skill for many children—but it also causes a regression in both thinking and behavior. Thus, an angry five-year-old tends to think and act like a two-year-old, an eight-year-old like a five-year-old, and so on. Given such regression in the face of anger, one of the most significant problems with angry interchanges between parent and child is that the child *does not— cannot—learn anything from angry interchanges.* Most parents intend that the confrontation teach their child a lesson, or contribute to molding her behavior. Anger, however, has the opposite effect: the child learns nothing.

3. *Parents' angry outbursts give attention to their children—that is, to their misbehaving children.* Giving attention reinforces behavior; removing or withholding attention achieves the opposite. When parents are angry, they can put on quite a show! They may shout, scream, and get red in the face. They may flail their arms or even give a spanking. However they display their anger, at such times 100 percent of their attention is focused on the child. While it is unquestionably unpleasant, their anger provides abundant attention and hence reinforcement to the child's misbehavior. In essence, parents' anger acts like water and food to nourish the child's undesirable behavior, when in reality, drought and starvation are required to bring it to a timely end.

4. *Parents who have an angry interaction with their child often feel both incompetent and guilty.* They feel distraught and foolish for having allowed themselves to become riled. They understand that their anger does not set a good example, so they also feel bad when they say hurtful things. Once calm, they realize that the punishments they have meted out in the heat of the moment may be completely unenforceable and thus cannot accomplish the disciplinary goal. Parents also feel miserable because they believe they have made their child feel bad. Whether the child is still storming with anger or crying with unhappiness, he displays feelings the parents do not want to have caused.

Many parents assume that through an angry interchange they have made their child feel guilty. For a young child, this is probably an inaccurate assumption. Until the stage of development that occurs at about age ten, a child cannot reflect objectively on himself as an actor in a situation. Without this ability—especially when his thinking is hindered by anger—a young child does not inflict guilt on himself. So he does not walk away from an angry interchange with his parents saying, "I'm such a bad child. How could I have behaved this way toward my parent?" Instead, he just continues to be angry. Even if the child actually feels no guilt, however, most conscientious parents still feel miserable about an interaction that caused their child distress.

Oh, what a tangled web we weave with anger! The angry parent provides the wrong model. The angry child cannot process the intended lesson. The parent gives the child the wrong kind of attention—but abundant attention nonetheless—and thus reinforces the wrong kind of behavior. The parent feels miserable and guilty. And in the end, anger does not achieve the desired outcome: the child's good behavior.

AT TWO, SAMMY was an energetic little boy. He often plowed through the house at full speed with his favorite teddy bear in tow, upsetting whatever came into his still-clumsy path. His mother tried patiently to enforce a rule: "Walk in the house; run outside." But with a fussy infant to care for in addition to Sammy, and long days on her own while her husband was away on business, she found her fuse growing shorter every day.

One day Sammy ran into the coffee table yet again and, flailing his stuffed bear, broke a vase. Susan lost it. She shouted, "You're a bad, bad boy. I told you not to run in the house. Now go sit in your room. Teddy stays with me."

"No, no!" shrieked Sammy. "Bad Mommy. Teddy go me."

Susan picked up Sammy, turned him over her knee, and spanked him hard. "That's it, Sammy. I'm taking Teddy and you're never getting him back."

Angry and inconsolable, Sammy alternately screamed and sobbed, struggling to catch his breath. Susan immediately felt guilty for her outburst, cuddled Sammy, and gave him back his beloved bear.

If such angry exchanges were repeated very often, Sammy would soon learn how to get his own way and get plenty of attention from his mother: have a tantrum.

The Outcome of Angry Interchanges: Misbehaving Children

For all these reasons, *anger does not work as a discipline technique.* Whatever other effect it may have, anger does not succeed in causing repeated good behavior for the long term. Instead, anger itself becomes an expectation.

The bigger consequence of letting anger reign, however, is that children fail to learn how to manage either their emotions or their behavior. For instance, if Sammy and his mother fell into a pattern of angry interchanges, he would fail to learn how to control his temper and follow rules. Instead, he would learn to explode, and to exploit both his tantrums and others' feelings.

Without gaining the experience of managing their emotions and solving problems rationally early in life, children will lack both the motivation and the skills required to regulate their responses to various situations as they grow through the preteen and teen years and into adulthood. Especially during the preadult years, they will experience the ebb and flow of their own emotions and also will be assaulted by influences from countless external sources. Many such situations will require them to manage their anger. The only way they can become equipped for these times is to form the right habits earlier in life.

Children learn how to manage their emotions and make wise decisions through discipline that is administered fairly, calmly, and consistently throughout childhood. The practices parents employ with their children shape habits that will serve the children well when faced with trying situations during teenage and adulthood. Thus, for many reasons, as parents struggle through the difficult moments, they need to hold firmly to a consistent discipline approach and to avoid using anger as a discipline technique. Fortunately, the techniques in this book can help parents navigate even the toughest times with fairness, consistency, firmness, and relative calm. Using these techniques, parents can bring about the desired results in their children's present and future behavior. Read on.

3

Consequences: The Foundation for Discipline

> I truly believe that for Jessica to grow up to be a responsible adult, I must provide a foundation in good discipline now. But gosh! It's a whole lot easier said than done, day after day.

How often I hear words like these—and no wonder! Being "responsible" is rooted in making appropriate decisions, and discipline is one of the major ways that parents help their children learn to make good decisions. Because very young children do not yet have the ability to use reason in making choices, they act largely on impulse as they respond to almost limitless options.

Initially, parents simply make decisions for their babies. But as children grow, parents begin more and more to guide the children's ability to make decisions. Parents' first influences on their children's decision-making process are essentially examples with explanations: parents structure the environment to ensure their children's safety and well-being, and they also make decisions on their children's behalf. As the children acquire mobility and language, parents expand beyond their initial measures. They begin to establish rules, and they teach their children about "right and wrong" or "good and bad" choices.

Around age three, children acquire some ability to become "intentional" about their behavior—that is, they can make deliberate choices rather than just react on instinct. At this point in their development, they can understand that their decisions have consequences, and they begin to make choices based on that understanding. As they further develop this ability throughout their childhood and teen years, they continue to need the structure, guidance, discipline, and support their parents provide.

To develop control over their own behavior, children need to understand consequences.

- If-then thinking provides the rational basis for understanding the consequences of their actions.
- The 4 Cs—the consistent use of clear, contingent consequences—provide the framework for behaving with intention.
- In disciplining children, parents' most powerful consequence is their own attention.

This chapter is devoted to several aspects of consequences, which form the very *foundation for discipline*. Whether discipline is externally imposed by parents or self-managed by the child, its success depends on understanding the consequences of one's actions. Understanding how consequences operate is particularly important to this book because consequences form the basis for the discipline techniques explained in the following chapters.

This chapter addresses three fundamental concepts:

1. the use of *if-then thinking* as a process of predicting outcomes
2. the use of consequences to influence behavior, specifically in a context I call the *4 Cs*—the consistent use of clear, contingent consequences
3. the most powerful consequence of all: *parents' attention*

By teaching if-then thinking to their children, and by consistently using clear, contingent consequences, parents provide their children with the ability and context to make appropriate decisions. By giving or withdrawing their own attention as part of a consistent discipline plan, parents use the single most potent consequence at their disposal—and thus they can exert powerful influence over their children's behavior.

If-Then Thinking: The Basis for Responsible Decision Making

If-then thinking is the logical foundation for making prudent choices. As adults, we use it constantly, though quite often subconsciously, to help guide our behavior. By using if-then thinking, we apply logic to options. As a result, we can understand and weigh the probable outcomes, or consequences, of various alternatives.

In teaching children if-then thinking, the parents' first goal is to help children understand *the connection between their own behavior and the consequences that result from it.* Children learn to manage their behavior as they grow to understand that *appropriate behavior* will produce *positive* outcomes, whereas *misbehavior* will result in *negative* outcomes. In order to become responsible adults, they must acquire this essential skill of if-then thinking and practice it until it becomes second nature.

Children begin life with no ability whatsoever to make reasoned choices about their behavior. As they grow, so does their ability to make appropriate decisions, and parents play a crucial role in helping children develop this ability. Of course, most parents' paramount goal is for their children to mature into adults who can make sound choices and regulate their behavior entirely on their own. So between their children's infancy and adulthood comes parenting—a lot of parenting! One of the most critical aspects of that parenting is to help children learn how to make increasingly complex decisions about their behavior.

If-then thinking lies at the very heart of learning to make sound decisions about our own behavior. This particular type of logic enables us to understand and reliably predict outcomes: *if* I make this choice, *then* this will be the likely consequence. Once children are taught the concept of if-then thinking, they need to internalize and repeat this mental process so often that it becomes a habit of mind. When their ability to perform if-then thinking has become virtually automatic, they are finally equipped to make desirable choices about their behavior most of the time.

Although children can learn to predict some outcomes through their own trial and error, they can acquire this skill better and faster if their parents, teachers, and other caregivers very deliberately teach them if-then thinking and help them practice and refine it. Continuous repetition of the if-then model is required in order for children to develop the understanding that every action likely has consequences—good or bad—and that some consequences are more serious and important than others.

For most adults, if-then thinking is so deeply ingrained that we seldom consider how frequently we use it to make choices. In reality, adults use it constantly, rapidly, and almost subconsciously. For example, when we are running late for an appointment, how heavily we tread on the accelerator is actually the product of multiple *if-then* considerations; most of these are so ingrained as to require little conscious thought. But at some earlier points, we had to learn to recognize and evaluate multiple possibilities: *If* the roads are slick, *then* the car might skid, resulting in an accident. *If* traffic is heavy, *then* driving fast might require weaving in and out of lanes; *if* other drivers are not paying careful attention to our weaving, *then* they might run into us. *If* a bicyclist weaves into our path when we are traveling fast, *then* we may not have sufficient time or control to dodge around him. *If* the police are patrolling, *then* we may get a ticket. *If*, on the other hand, the roads are dry, the traffic is light, we do not drive through areas where bicyclists frequently ride, and the road is not heavily patrolled, *then* the possibility of negative outcomes is lessened, and we may choose to drive faster.

If . . . then, if . . . then, if . . . then . . . on and on we spin rapidly through seemingly endless lists of possibilities and consequences. Driving a car is a routine matter, yet we continuously make rather complex decisions while driving. For most of these decisions, we use if-then logic in the context of our experience and knowledge, which allows us to consider multiple sets of consequences. Driving is only one example, but it reveals how we govern our adult behavior every day. We constantly go through complex—but frequently automatic and subconscious—mental acrobatics to examine choices and reflect on possible consequences.

Children are not born equipped to perform these complex intellectual gymnastics, but they begin making decisions at an early age. Thus, the challenge for parents is how to teach their children if-then thinking at a time and in a way that best prepares them to make responsible decisions.

The most opportune time for teaching and reinforcing if-then thinking is when children are in the early stages of developing their ability to use reason: at about two and a half or three years old. From then on, children can learn to regulate their behavior if they can accurately predict the outcomes or consequences associated with it.

Although it is ultimately beneficial for parents to model if-then thinking out loud and repeatedly when their children are very young, they cannot reasonably expect little ones to apply it themselves until they are older. *For children under age three, parents will be far less frustrated if they distract or remove a child from a forbidden temptation.* This is particularly important for those behaviors that are either dangerous (touching the hot stove), destructive (breaking the stereo), or antisocial (hitting, shoving, kicking).

Children of ages three and four increasingly can inhibit a few impulses. (See the Appendix for an explanation of skills children acquire at various stages of development.) It is unreasonable for parents to tell a two-year-old, "Don't touch the TV," and expect her to leave it alone—especially when she is alone in the room with it. She cannot use language well enough yet to reason that if she touches the TV, then she will get in trouble. By age four, however, that same child will be able to understand this simple cause-and-effect logic. Thus, at this age, she can follow directions most of the time, even without constant monitoring.

As children develop their cognitive abilities between ages four and six, they become able to make some predictions about outcomes and based on these predictions, they can inhibit some of their impulses. As these abilities are developing, parents have an ideal opportunity to teach children if-then thinking repeatedly and consistently. At this stage, children are well able to understand and apply if-then thinking in certain repetitive situations. *During this developmental stage, parents can help their children greatly by articulating aloud the thought processes of decision making.* As children prepare to make decisions, parents can guide them through the repetitive if-then thought process of prediction: *If* you were to do this, *then* what do you think would happen? What else might you choose to do? *If* you were to do that instead, *then* what do you think the outcome would be? Which outcome do you prefer? Which would be a better decision?

As they grow older, children become increasingly able to use more sophisticated logic and to reason their way through more complex issues. A nine-year-old, for example, can understand that *if* he throws a baseball wildly, *then* it might break the neighbor's window, or it might roll into the street, or it might hit somebody. *If* he breaks a window, *then* the neighbor might get mad, and Mom would probably make him earn money to pay for it. He can anticipate more than one further consequence for each of the possible consequences of his wild throw. With a child at this and more advanced stages of development, the parents' job of teaching if-then thinking takes on new dimensions. They can teach increasingly complex reasoning skills as their children grow in the ability to understand and apply those skills.

Besides helping the children learn to apply if-then thinking to their independent decision making, it is very important that parents also help children apply such logic to their own behavior, in the context of discipline. The application of the 4 Cs is a particularly effective way to help children understand the connection between their own behavior and its consequences: if I hit my sister, then Mom will punish me. My behavior does have a consequence.

The 4 Cs: Consistent Use of Clear, Contingent Consequences

What a mouthful! Yet if I could give all parents just two gifts, the very first would be the 4 Cs. The second would be an understanding of the power inherent in giving and withdrawing their attention. Together, these principles form a very powerful foundation for discipline. The understanding of—and the ability to apply—these principles provides the essential context for all of the discipline techniques in the chapters to follow.

Children find it easiest to learn to behave when they fully understand what is expected of them, when they know what consequence will occur if they perform or fail to perform accordingly, and when the consequence for the behavior is the same every single time. This is the 4 Cs principle—*the consistent use of clear, contingent consequences*. This all-important structure makes the world a comfortable place for children and provides them with a context for making sound choices.

It is easiest to grasp the concept of the 4 Cs by understanding how each term is defined in this context, beginning with *consequences*.

Consequences

Newton's third law of motion states that for every action, there is an equal and opposite reaction. The laws of human behavior are not quite so quantifiable nor, alas, predictable. Nonetheless, it certainly seems true that for every human action, there is some consequence. That consequence may be positive, negative, or neutral in its impact, but as adults understand, human behavior always produces some reaction.

This concept of consequences is what children need to learn as a first step toward regulating their own behavior. Even before they are able to absorb and use *if-then* thinking in an abstract way, they can be taught that there are consequences for their own behaviors.

At the most fundamental level, young children need to learn that *if* they behave appropriately, *then* there will be a positive consequence. Conversely, *if* they behave inappropriately, *then* there will be another kind of consequence. As they develop greater cognitive skills, children can learn to apply if-then thinking and the

EARLY IN MY career, I worked with a group of boys who had been diagnosed with behavior disorders. I was struck by the fact that these youngsters almost always acted solely on the basis of their own impulses or desires and could not regulate their own behavior. In treating them, our team devised a very rigid and elaborate system of token reinforcements—highly specific consequences—for each child. Through that experience, I grew very curious about how some children learn to regulate their own behavior while others do not.

That curiosity spurred me later on to conduct some research on how children decide to do chores—tasks they do not particularly want to do—in the absence of highly formalized reward and punishment systems. I theorized that parents' consistent use of clear, contingent consequences—both positive and negative—would strongly influence their children's ability to manage their behavior. I thought that under these conditions, children could internalize rules, learn if-then thinking, and begin to behave appropriately. Eventually, they would be able to manage their behavior without the external consequences. The study proved these very points.

Thus, a seven-year-old boy learned to make his bed every morning—a chore he thoroughly disliked—because he learned that if he did, he would be allowed to watch TV that evening, and if he did not, then he would watch no TV that day. Within several months, making the bed became an automatic part of his daily routine, and the rigid system of consequences for that chore was no longer needed.

concept of consequences to their own decision making. Ultimately, this pattern of thought is what allows them to grow into responsible adults.

Parents teach their children how to behave by establishing expectations and rules, and by attaching consequences to these. If the child behaves according to the expectations and rules, then the consequences are positive. If the child disobeys or acts contrary to the rules and expectations, then the consequences are not positive.

Contingent

Contingent consequences are those that *directly follow and only follow* certain behaviors. Psychologists use the phrase "contingency management of behavior" to refer to a prescriptive system in which parents, teachers, and children themselves promote desirable behaviors or inhibit undesirable ones through reinforcement. The concept of reinforcement is explained more fully in Chapter 4. For now, suffice it to say that a contingent consequence is one that corresponds to—or is, in a sense, attached to—a certain defined behavior.

For instance, if a parent wants to teach his child to pick up her toys before dinner, he might assign a positive consequence for doing that chore. Each time the child picks up her toys without being asked more than once, Dad praises her and puts a sticker on her job chart. Each time the child fails to pick up her toys when asked, Dad explains that she did not do what she was supposed to, and therefore she will get no sticker that day. The same consequence is assigned to the same behavior, repeatedly. Thus, it is a *contingent* consequence: a direct, predictable correlation is made between a behavior and a consequence.

Consistent

Now here is a word that needs no definition! Yet, it is probably the toughest "C" of the bunch for parents to put into practice.

ROGER WAS AN out-of-control, angry eight-year-old. His parents found him a constant challenge, and his teachers complained that he was immature, unable to follow directions, and often badly behaved. They questioned whether he might have attention deficit disorder (ADD), and suggested the parents discuss his behavior with his pediatrician, who then sent the parents to me.

I asked his parents to help me piece together an understanding of what Roger had been like up to this point. They described him as a very independent child, from infancy on. Like virtually all children, he had temper tantrums when he was two. Unlike other children, however, he never stopped having them.

When I began asking about how they dealt with his tantrums and misbehavior, a pattern emerged. Roger's parents typically tried explaining to him how they expected him to behave; when that did not work, they switched to scolding him; and when that did not succeed, they tried bribing him. They continued this pattern—constantly changing their reactions to his misdeeds, hoping to find the magic formula. As a result, both they and Roger were almost constantly confused, and his misbehavior had become a way of life.

I asked the parents to set a few critical goals for Roger's behavior. They were to assign a positive consequence for meeting each goal, which would not be awarded if Roger failed to meet the goal. At a quiet time when he was behaving well, they were to explain the new system to him and tell him what the consequence would be for each behavior. Then they were to stick to it without fail.

continued

> They called me two weeks later. They felt as though they had a different child. The change in Roger's behavior was dramatic. His behavior was greatly improved, and he was a much happier boy.
>
> What had changed? They were setting expectations and consistently applying the same contingent consequences. It made all the difference.

The application of a contingent consequence is effective only if it is used consistently, time after time after time. This is because children cannot calculate the odds of a rule being enforced, nor can they foresee the various rationales that may underlie exceptions. In order to live by a rule, they need to rely on consequences that are consistent and therefore predictable. So if a parent sends a child to his room seven times out of ten for talking back, but does not enforce this consequence the other three times, then in the child's mind, there is no contingent consequence. He has learned that sometimes he will be sent to his room and sometimes he will not. Thus, he cannot make the connection that talking back results consistently in the same negative consequence. Under these circumstances, the child is likely to behave according to his impulses or desires, rather than to consider any consequences.

There are a thousand and one extremely understandable reasons why contingent consequences may not be administered consistently. At home, parents may set up the contingent consequence and follow through, but Grandma does not impose the same consequence when the child is at her house. Or the child may talk back in the grocery store when Mom is in a rush to get home. Or the parent is tired or distracted and just does not take the time and energy to administer the consequence consistently. In each of these situations, alas, there is no *consistent* consequence.

GEORGE AND SHARI were very frustrated. Bedtime for their nine-year-old daughter had become a nightly battle. The rule required Amanda to turn off the TV at 8:30 p.m. and be in bed at 9:00 p.m. Lately, she had argued over turning off the TV, dawdled while getting herself ready, and whined that her parents were unfair when they made her go to bed.

Her parents were perturbed because they tried so hard to be very fair and lenient enough to allow exceptions they thought were in her best interests. For instance, they did allow Amanda to watch until 9:00 p.m. or even later if an educational program was on TV. Sometimes, they even let her watch an extra fifteen minutes or so of anything she wanted to watch.

So why the problem? In their desire to provide structure, George and Shari had established a reasonable rule—but then failed to apply it consistently. Amanda could not count on the rule being enforced, so she played the odds in her own favor—to stay up later.

Clear

Like *consistent*, the term *clear* needs no definition. But it does deserve a context. When establishing a contingent consequence, a parent needs to be sure that the child fully understands what behavior is expected of her, and what consequence will occur if she does not meet that expectation. Sometimes, even though parents are very clear in their own minds about what behaviors they are trying to regulate and what consequences they will effect, these behaviors and consequences may not be equally as clear to their children.

Two issues are generally at work here. First, children, particularly bright children, have a way of seeming to understand when they actually do not. When asked, "Do you understand what I'm telling you?" they may nod their heads and even say yes. But they may not really understand how to translate "not talking back" or other more complex expectations into their own behavior.

Sometimes this is because the parents fail to explain the expectation or the consequence very clearly. But more often, parents give an explanation that is clear to an adult but *too complicated for the child at a particular age*. Parents will always be most successful if they explain both the desired behavior and the consequence for misbehaving in a way that corresponds to the child's developmental age.

For example, in the case of a child who loves to play with a forbidden object such as the TV remote control, at twenty months he would be developmentally unable to act on his father's directive not to touch. The same child at age four would be able to resist touching the remote if his father explained to him in very simple words that he was never to touch it. If his father also explained that the TV would be turned off immediately whenever the child touched the remote, then the child would understand the consequence. If Dad carried out this contingent consequence consistently every time the little boy disobeyed, he would soon learn not to touch the remote.

The 4 Cs are a package of concepts that parents, teachers, and caregivers can use to structure discipline. As with most challenges of parenting, the 4 Cs are far easier to describe than to apply day after day. With thoughtful reflection, however, parents almost always can analyze their discipline issues and figure out how to resolve them using the 4 Cs. By understanding how they use—or fail to use—clear, consistent, contingent consequences, parents can soon make effective changes in their discipline techniques. These changes, in turn, yield the behaviors they want to bring about in their children. When parents commit to using this fun-

WHEN STAN WENT to kindergarten, he discovered wise-cracks. On the playground, people laughed at some of his friends' expressions, so he started to adopt them.

When he first said them at home, Mom spoke sharply to him each time he made a rude remark. "Stop the wise-cracks," she would say. But Stan kept on, each day bringing home a new unacceptable phrase.

Finally, Mom sat down with him at a quiet moment. "Stan," she said, "you and I need to talk about something. You know I sometimes tell you to stop the wisecracks. I wonder if you really understand what that means and why I want you to stop."

Stan said he thought *wisecrack* meant saying something funny. He also really did not understand why his mother got mad at him for saying the same wisecracks that made his friends laugh.

Mom then explained that the expressions "Oh yeah?" and "Gee, you're dumb!" were wisecracks. She told him that even though some of his friends at school said such things and other people laughed, the reason she did not want him to say them was because they could hurt people's feelings. "I think you really like your teachers, family, and friends, don't you?" Stan nodded vigorously. "If you like them, then you need to talk in a way that shows them that you like them. You want to show them respect. When you use wisecracks, it sounds like you want to be mean to them. So from now on, before you use an expression like that, stop and think about how it would make someone feel. And if you are not sure, don't use it or come and ask me about it."

continued

Stan now began to understand the difference. From then on, he seldom used wisecracks, and he did ask his mom about some new words he heard at school. By explaining clearly what a wisecrack was and how she expected Stan to behave, the problem was solved—even without using consequences.

damental approach, they almost unfailingly are delighted to find that their children behave well much of the time.

Later chapters will explain some fundamental behavioral concepts and four discipline techniques—two that use specific, tangible consequences to influence children's behavior, and two that rely on the withdrawal of parents' attention. Most important, all of these techniques (even one that uses a tangible reward system) ultimately hinge on using parents' attention as a consequence for behavior.

Parents' Attention: The Most Powerful Consequence

"Mommy, Mommy, watch me!" This is every young child's mantra, repeated over and over again during the early years and implied, if not overtly spoken, during the growing-up years that follow. Young children want their parents' attention above all else. They come into this world prepared to attach themselves to other human beings, and very soon they perceive attention to themselves as something positive. For the vast majority of children— those who love and are loved by their parents—getting their parents to pay attention to them is one of the mainstays of their lives. Parents' attention has enormous importance for children

every single minute, hour, and day—and it never loses that importance. *Thus, the most powerful consequence parents can use to influence
their children's behavior is the way in which the parents give or withdraw
their attention.*

There are many theories about the impact of parents' attention
on children's self-esteem, learning, and other aspects of their lives.
While parents' behavior unquestionably influences many aspects
of their children's lives, this book will focus solely on one aspect:
the deliberate use of parents' attention as a critical discipline technique.
This attention is parents' most potent and effective "tool" to help
children learn to regulate their own behavior.

In this context, parents' attention is a direct consequence—a
part of the 4-Cs system. In their ongoing efforts to teach their
children self-discipline, parents usually have a short list of goals
they are working toward at any given time. Often these emerge

---

WHEN I ASK parents, "What is the most powerful discipline
technique you use?" they almost always answer with negatives: taking away privileges, sending the child to her
room, grounding her, and sometimes spanking or hitting
her. Generally, though, the parents are in my office because
the very techniques they have just described are not working, and they are quick to say so. They know these techniques are failing them, but they do not know what else
to try.

In reality, none of these long-established discipline techniques are nearly as powerful as parents deliberately and consistently giving or withdrawing their own attention. Once
parents learn how to do this, they are inevitably amazed and
thrilled with the results.

without conscious attention, such as when the child begins to display a new behavior and parents respond somewhat automatically. In the 4-Cs approach, parents become more deliberate. They define and communicate rules and expectations, and assign a clear, specific consequence to each behavior with an understanding of how they will apply the consequence consistently.

Giving Attention

In assigning a consequence to a behavioral goal, parents find that the most effective reward they can give for their child's good behavior is simply noticing and responding. Many parents ask, "Why should I praise my child just for doing what he's supposed to do?" This is a very reasonable question. After all, parents can expect that as their children approach adulthood, they will be able to regulate their own behavior most of the time without constant reminders. It is logical for parents to worry that their children might come to expect constant praise, or conversely, not learn to behave well without it.

But the answer lies in the nature of children; children *need* their parents' attention. So rather than allow good behavior to go unnoticed, parents will help ensure its recurrence by using a deliberate strategy of noticing and communicating their pleasure when their children do what is asked of them. Thus, for example, if a parent wants to eliminate or reduce her child's whining and begging, she will do well to remind him of how she expects him to behave *before* taking him into the grocery store, or *before* some other situation in which he tends to whine or beg. Once there, the parent is likely to preclude an unpleasant episode if she says early in the shopping trip, "You're behaving so well—just like we talked about. It makes me happy when you are pleasant and not whining or begging. Good for you!" As children grow older, they will not require their parents' praise quite so frequently in order to manage their behavior. But if the correlation between good behavior and parents' attention has been established early on, parents will find that maintaining the habit holds them in good stead. A quick smile or word of praise in recognition of good behavior will yield more of the same, with far less need for the negative side of discipline.

Withdrawing Attention

Withdrawing attention is practiced less than giving attention. Many of the parents I see in my office actually give their children plenty of attention—but far too much of it for negative behaviors. A widening spiral of emotion and attention typically occurs in response to a misdeed. Often such a spiral results in parents' anger and children's continuing misbehavior and frustration with themselves. As with Dan, many parents respond to their children's misdeed by escalating from an initial quiet reminder to repeated, noisy, contentious interactions. What has happened in these circumstances? The child has received attention—a lot of attention!—for behaving badly. If parents repeatedly give their child attention in response to undesirable behavior, they will perpetuate that behavior.

So what is the alternative to such a vicious cycle? One that I highly recommend is Cool Down—a technique similar to the one commonly called Time-Out, described in Chapter 7. But Cool Down has some significant differences from Time-Out. There are two fundamental reasons for the success of Cool Down, and these are different from some versions of Time Out. First, parents make very clear to the child exactly which behavior has caused this consequence to be invoked. Second, *they immediately and completely withdraw their attention.* They do not interact with the child during that specified period of time, and the child is made to understand that she must not misbehave—or try to get her parents'

DAN IS AN intelligent, successful man in his thirties. Respected for his skills as a trial lawyer, he is a good listener, discerning judge of character, and gifted legal strategist.

As he talked about his five-year-old, however, his manner reflected real anguish. "I start by being patient, but I always wind up screaming. I tell him the same thing ten times, but he just won't behave until I yell at him. If he just did what I told him the first time, I wouldn't have to get angry. But he always makes me go to the extreme."

I tested his logic. "So," I asked, "if screaming is the only technique that works, why don't you just begin by screaming at your son each time he misbehaves?" Dan looked startled. Why would an intelligent man do such a foolish thing? Then it hit him. He was, in effect, doing exactly that: he was using anger to send his son the message, "I'm serious." He was repeatedly giving his son a lot of attention as a consequence—but for the wrong behavior. He had established a pattern that was not working. It never would work.

With this perspective, he was ready to undertake a new system of discipline. He soon learned to withdraw his attention, instead of scream, when his son misbehaved. But soon, even this became less necessary, because he also made his expectations clearer and praised his son whenever the boy behaved as he was asked to.

attention—for a specified period of time prior to the end of her Cool Down. Thus, instead of giving their child attention for misbehaving, parents clearly and deliberately withdraw their attention. In order to regain her parents' attention, the child must comply with the rule or expectation. In other words, she gets attention only when she behaves well, and this attention reinforces her good behavior.

Whether using the specific Cool Down technique or not, parents can apply the general principle of giving their attention as a consequence of their child's desirable behavior and withdrawing it as a consequence of her undesirable behavior. Withdrawing attention is most effective if invoked in the context of a discipline plan, and less effective outside of such a plan. In the 4-Cs system of discipline, however, this technique can exert as much power in terminating an undesirable behavior as positive attention can in encouraging a desirable one. Giving and withdrawing attention are two sides of the same coin, and both sides yield interest in children's behavioral bank accounts.

The word *discipline* often connotes reaction against negative behavior. In reality, however, parents have daily opportunities to use discipline—a set of clear, contingent consequences applied consistently—to help their children learn how to regulate their own behavior. By thoughtfully and consistently using their own attention as the most critical consequence of all, parents help their children to develop the kind of if-then thinking that allows them to make sound choices about their behavior. In such a structure, and with such parents, children are happier and better behaved during their growing-up years, and they become the independent, responsible adults that their parents have hoped for.

4

The Four Behavioral Principles of Discipline

> My mother-in-law says I'm spoiling my son. My neighbor says you can never give a child too much love and attention. The experts I see on TV all have their own methods for disciplining kids—and they don't agree with each other. How am I supposed to figure out what to do?

It is no surprise that parents feel overwhelmed by the amount of child-rearing advice that regularly assails them, and hence are somewhat bewildered about the "right" way to discipline their children. If only there were some magic formula! Then all parents would know exactly what to do, and all children would be perfectly behaved all the time. Alas, as a society we are not quite there yet.

Some methods of discipline, however, are far more effective than others. These reduce frustration for both parents and children, and elicit better behavior from children on a fairly consistent basis. How can parents determine which discipline techniques will result in these desirable outcomes? One way is to assess them against some well-established principles based on a widely accepted theory called *Behaviorism.*

This theory was first advanced by B. F. Skinner and other psychologists from the 1930s through the 1960s. During that time, Skinner and his colleagues believed that behaviorism provided a rationale for all human behavior. In its simplest terms, the theory of behaviorism states that all human behaviors are learned. Early behavioral psychologists hypothesized that humans develop all of their life skills because they are "taught" them, either directly or indirectly. Later, research by other psychologists demonstrated that behaviorism could not fully account for the development of all human behaviors. For instance, the process of acquiring language has been proven to be complex, involving genetic components as well as learning. Extensive research has shown, however, that four fundamental principles of behaviorism can influence individuals to change their behavior. These have become so widely accepted that they are considered as fact. The four fundamental ways to modify a behavior are

1. positive reinforcement
2. negative reinforcement
3. extinction
4. punishment

Two of these, positive reinforcement and negative reinforcement, are ways to increase the occurrence of a behavior. The other two, extinction and punishment, decrease the likelihood that a behavior will recur.

With these four principles, parents have a sound rationale for evaluating the various discipline techniques proposed by experts—whether psychologists or mothers-in-law!—and for analyzing their own daily interactions with their children. In fact, these principles form the basis for the discipline techniques described in the remaining chapters of this book.

Positive Reinforcement

In behavioral terms, the word *reinforcement* always means a technique that increases the likelihood that a behavior will be repeated. When parents want to encourage their children to perform a particular good behavior more frequently, they use positive reinforcement. In fact, most parents use positive reinforcement with their children quite often and quite naturally.

Positive reinforcement encourages the repetition of a desirable behavior by following it with a reward—either tangible or social.

The logic of positive reinforcement is straightforward: *when people want to encourage an individual to repeat a "good" behavior, they reward that behavior with something pleasurable.* In many households and work situations, positive reinforcement is deeply embedded as a way of life. "What a great dinner! I really enjoyed that!" says one spouse to another. Now the cook is far more likely to repeat the success. "You really did a great job on your paper. It was a tough assignment, but you researched and analyzed it well, and you added excellent ideas of your own," says the teacher. As a result, the student will probably research, analyze, and add creative ideas in future papers to earn such praise again. In business, bonuses for "hitting the numbers" are constructed to reward success. At home, parents clap for the toddler's first steps, crow over each new word a five-year-old learns to read, and double the teacher's reinforcement when the teenager brings home an A on a term paper. Every day, in hundreds of ways, people use positive words and deeds to reinforce desirable actions and thereby increase the probability that those actions will occur again.

Psychologists generally distinguish between two types of positive reinforcement: *social reinforcement* and *tangible reinforcement.* Although there are other ways of classifying positive responses, these two serve as a practical way of thinking about them.

Social reinforcement is a means of encouraging the repetition of a behavior solely through a verbal or physical response to it. It comes in many familiar varieties. Praise, a compliment, a pat on the back, a squeeze on the arm, a hug—all of these are social reinforcements. These actions typically are performed in a warm and caring manner that adds to their impact on the recipient. As a result, such social reinforcements encourage the recipient to repeat the behavior that was rewarded. Most people use positive social reinforcements frequently and naturally, and have an innate understanding of how these reinforcements reward desirable behaviors and encourage their repetition.

In some situations, however, social reinforcement alone may not be sufficient to increase a desired behavior. For example, learning a new behavior that requires a complete change of an existing habit—like potty training or quitting smoking—may be more successful when it is encouraged by additional means.

Those additional forms of positive reinforcement usually fall in the realm of tangible rewards. These are concrete items that can be seen and touched (like candy or a toy) or experiences (such as a trip to the playground) that serve as treats. Parents often have mixed or even negative feelings about tangible reinforcements. Some think they seem like bribes and have some negative connotations of "buying" good behavior. Others say they simply don't work. Depending on the way in which tangible reinforcements are used, both opinions can be true; that is, tangible reinforcements do have the quality of a business transaction in "buying" good behavior, and they also may be ineffective in changing a behavior. In many circumstances, however, tangible rewards can be used very effectively to influence behavior. The success of positive reinforcement using tangible rewards often depends on having a system and a clear purpose for administering them.

Negative Reinforcement

The term *negative reinforcement* is frequently misused, even by psychologists. It is often confused with punishment (see the last section of this chapter), but there are some fundamental differences. The critical difference between negative reinforcement and punishment is suggested by the word *reinforcement*, which is defined as a means to increase the likelihood of a behavior reoccurring. *Negative reinforcement is defined as removing something undesirable in order to encourage an individual to repeat a particular behavior.*

When a behavior is followed by the removal of something unpleasant, the behavior is negatively reinforced.

So how does negative reinforcement apply to parenting? This type of reinforcement does play a role in child discipline, but more often than not, it is misused and causes the opposite of the desired outcome. Negative reinforcement typically occurs without forethought, and its effect is usually unintended. Thus, it is especially important for parents to recognize when negative reinforcement is occurring and to intervene and prevent it.

In many families, it is actually the child who provides negative reinforcement and thereby encourages the parent to repeat a behavior, rather than the reverse. It is not at all uncommon for a child to control a confrontation, as in the example on the next page. In such a situation, the child persists in misbehaving while the parent

JIM DREADED THE shouting match that had become a part of his daily parenting routine. It always began when he asked Greg to turn off the TV and come to dinner. He began with a polite directive, which escalated from "Now, Greg. Turn it off now, please," to "I said to turn off that TV and I meant it! Now turn it off this instant or I'll give you something to cry about!" Throughout every encounter, Greg always ignored his father until he was red-faced and shouting. Then the boy would shrug, click it off, and silently come to the table.

By suddenly stopping his disobedience when his father's anger reached its peak, Greg negatively reinforced his father's escalating anger. Once Jim figured out that he was the one whose behavior was being managed by his child, he was able to stop the cycle and adopt a more successful discipline approach.

repeats an instruction over and over, becoming louder and angrier at each reiteration. Only after she is given numerous angry commands does the child finally comply. By not ceasing her misbehavior until after her parent's anger has escalated, she effectively has promoted a repeat scenario. When she stops her negative conduct, she reinforces her parent's use of anger as a means of discipline.

In similar situations, it may be the parent who negatively reinforces a child's behavior, as in the following scenario. A parent and child are engaged in an angry exchange. Regardless of his mother's repeated demands and her mounting fury, the child refuses to comply with her instructions. Finally, the parent becomes frustrated and gives up. By withdrawing her anger while the child is still refusing to comply, the parent negatively reinforces his misbehavior. This encourages the child both to continue to misbehave now and to do so again, in the future.

Negative reinforcement is difficult to detect, let alone analyze, while it is occurring. Parents who find themselves too often caught up in angry confrontations may find it helpful to reflect on these situations during a quiet moment and consider whether they or their children are perpetuating undesirable behavior through negative reinforcement. With this understanding, they can then consider how to break the cycle. Negative reinforcement also serves an important role in fostering improved behavior in the context of the Cool Down technique, found in Chapter 7.

In summary, *both* forms of reinforcement, positive and negative, are behavioral tools of discipline. Whether parents' responses to their children's behavior are planned and deliberate, or spontaneous and unpremeditated, they always have some effect. One of the dangerous possibilities, as discussed in Chapter 2, is that anger can creep in as a destructive reinforcement "technique." Thus, parents benefit from understanding the concepts of positive and negative reinforcement, and from assessing what their responses—which act as reinforcement—teach their children about their own behavior.

Extinction

There are only two primary ways of increasing the repetition of a particular behavior (positive and negative reinforcement), and *only two ways of decreasing the incidence of that same behavior. The first method used to decrease the frequency of a behavior is* extinction; *the second is* punishment.

Extinction decreases the frequency of a behavior by providing no response to it at all.

SHORTLY AFTER SHE started first grade, Sallie started muttering things under her breath when she didn't get her way. Sometimes she'd grumble, "You are the meanest mother in the whole, wide world!" or even "I hate you!"

Her sensitive mother was both horrified and hurt to hear her daughter utter such harsh words. Her first instinct was to deal with Sallie's feelings and to talk with her about not saying such unpleasant things.

She was reassured to learn that, at age six, Sallie did not actually mean that she hated her mother or thought her mother was mean. At this stage in her development, she simply could not hold two conflicting thoughts together in her mind. She could not think, let alone say, "I love you, but right now I am really mad at you." So her anger came out through simpler expressions, often those she heard other children say at school.

Once her mother understood this, she decided that she could comfortably ignore the comments. Thus she chose to exercise extinction . . . and it worked. When Sallie's pronouncements stopped receiving any attention at all, she soon stopped muttering.

Both extinction and punishment can be very effective discipline techniques, but they are very different from each other. A technical term used by psychologists, *extinction* is the opposite of *reinforcement*. Whereas reinforcement encourages the repetition of a behavior by paying attention to it via giving some positive consequence or removing a negative consequence, *extinction helps reduce or eliminate the recurrence of a behavior by providing absolutely no response to it.*

Humans are hardwired to discontinue behaviors that yield no results. If we plant seeds but get no crops, we won't plant those seeds again. If we try a new diet but fail to lose weight, we will stop that diet. If we try to learn Japanese but can master only *arigato* and *sayonara*, we will soon quit trying. The logic is clear, and a substantial body of research also compellingly demonstrates that extinction is the most powerful way to decrease a behavior. One reason for its success is that extinction stimulates less of a reaction than does punishment.

In child discipline, extinction essentially translates into ignoring a behavior. When parents ignore a particular behavior, that behavior generally disappears in short order. The child does not get angry or upset, as he might if he were punished for the same behavior. He stops doing it because it fails to get his parents' attention.

There is, however, one very important requirement for extinction to work: it must be applied consistently. Thus, before deciding to ignore a particular behavior, the parent must clearly determine whether he can continue to ignore it. Otherwise, the parent is in danger of suddenly switching from extinction to reinforcement when he cannot tolerate the child's behavior anymore. For example, a child may beg for a treat at the grocery store. Repetition is in the very nature of begging. At first, the parent may be determined to ignore persistent wheedling, but finally he becomes frustrated and can no longer ignore it. At this point, he either gives in or gets angry. When this happens, the child's begging is not extinguished; instead, it is reinforced. Then guess what—on the next trip to the grocery store, the child will almost certainly beg again!

As a discipline technique, extinction can be particularly effective with behaviors that children employ specifically to get their parents' attention. Wheedling, slamming doors, and whining are prime examples. Since all of these behaviors are geared to getting a reaction, they are difficult for some parents to ignore. But if parents can ignore these behaviors *consistently*, the children soon realize that their ploy is not working, so they stop.

Once children are old enough to use if-then thinking, parents can increase the success of extinction by discussing with the children the consequences of their behavior. For instance, the parents may want to extinguish their daughter's whining. The first step is for them to sit down with her at a quiet time and explain that whining is a behavior they want her to stop doing. They lay out their plan: if she whines, then they will immediately turn their backs and ignore her. This explanation helps her to understand that her behavior produces consequences, and their follow-through with the stated extinction technique then discourages her whining by deliberately and consistently ignoring it. The system and the signal are made clear, and the child quickly learns from such teaching.

Before about age four, when children can understand and apply if-then reasoning, extinction can still be a useful, and even powerful, discipline technique. For instance, a toddler may throw a dish on the floor and laugh, thinking he has made a joke. If the parents or siblings enter into the joke, the child soon makes a habit of throwing food on the floor. If, however, a parent quietly puts the dish into the sink and the family goes on with other matters, the baby's "joke" is effectively ignored, and his food-throwing behavior is soon extinguished. In such circumstances, parents sometimes get flummoxed because toddlers can be very funny and very cute. In such situations, parents need to consider whether the behavior that is so adorable at age two will be equally adorable at age five. If the answer is no, then it is probably a behavior to extinguish.

Punishment

For most people, this is the word that first comes to mind when they think of discipline. Indeed, punishment has a place in the total scheme of discipline, but it is clearly not the only—or even the most effective—way to influence behavior.

Punishment means following a behavior with a negative consequence.

Simply defined, *punishment is applying a negative consequence to a behavior.* A behavior occurs and a negative outcome occurs immediately afterward, thereby reducing the likelihood that the behavior will be repeated. Parents generally think of punishment in terms of taking away privileges, scolding, or spanking. News stories contain dramatic examples of punishment every day—prison terms, beatings, and worse.

In fact, punishment is just feedback that arrives as an unpleasant consequence. For adults, speeding often results in a speeding ticket, overeating shows up as extra pounds on the scale, and an unpaid bill results in a threatening letter. Such consequences are important learning opportunities. These punishments provide critical information that helps people realize when they have done something wrong or inappropriate. As important as such information is for adults, it is even more important for children as they grow and learn. Children need feedback, both positive and negative, to make it clear to them which behaviors are acceptable and which are not.

As with any discipline technique, the goal for punishment is to effect a change in behavior, and this is accomplished most successfully when the punishment is administered without anger. Just as adults may react with anger when they are punished—whether with a speeding ticket or a prison sentence—children, too, sometimes react instinctively to punishment with anger. As described in Chapter 2, children cannot learn while they are mad, and parents often make poor decisions about discipline while angry.

For that reason, most psychologists agree that spanking and other forms of striking are not effective discipline techniques. Abundant research has shown that such punishment is generally both administered and received with anger. Studies have shown that children who are spanked tend to be more aggressive than those who are not—and that aggressiveness, in turn, leads to other undesirable behaviors.

In addition to minimizing anger, the other important factor in effective punishment is to ensure that, in the words of Sir William Gilbert's *Mikado*, "the punishment fit[s] the crime." Adults in this society may be unhappy about getting a speeding ticket, but they understand its rationale and generally see it as an appropriate consequence. If, however, their punishment were to have their offending accelerator foot chained to the floor for an extended period of time, they would likely become outraged.

Children have an even greater sensitivity to fairness and justice; so it is very important for parents to choose a punishment that the child will understand and accept as a meaningful and appropriate consequence of her behavior. By setting punishments in the context of learning tools, and administering punishments with fairness, parents can help their children learn to behave well. For example, if a three-year-old hurls a toy across the room, his parent may punish him by taking the toy away from him for the rest of the day. A seven-year-old who tears up her spelling paper may be required to rewrite the paper and write a note of apology to her teacher. Although both of these children may be temporarily upset, it is unlikely that they ultimately would feel their punishments were unfair.

The punishment and other discipline techniques that I recommend and explain in the next several chapters are designed to minimize anger—both the parent's and the child's—and to be administered in a way that is calm and fair. In particular, the Cool Down technique achieves results because it employs a sequence of punishment, then extinction, and then negative reinforcement. In order to be effective, all discipline techniques require thoughtful planning and consistent follow-through. This is the most certain way to ensure that the techniques have the effect of decreasing unwanted behaviors and increasing desirable ones.

Ah, the dream of perfectly behaved children—and all it takes is perfect discipline and perfect parenting! Fortunately, since most of us are mere mortals, there are some techniques that even we can use to produce good, if not entirely perfect, results. As it happens, the next chapter reveals some opportune information for us less-than-perfect humans.

Using Positive Reinforcement in a 4-Cs System of Discipline

I really try to praise my daughter a lot, and I give her treats when she earns them. Lately, some of her habits have been driving me crazy, though, and I wind up nagging. That doesn't feel right—there's got to be a better way.

Most parents give their children a lot of positive attention. They love them, they enjoy them, and they are proud of them. In response to such feelings, parents instinctively give their children hugs, praise, and treats. All of these translate into positive reinforcement, and children benefit greatly from living in an atmosphere of love and appreciation. Such spontaneous, uplifting responses are a way of life in many families.

In addition, some parents deliberately use positive reinforcement as a means of encouraging good behavior. Applying a concept advanced in many books on child rearing, many parents praise their children's effort rather than their specific actions. They show appreciation when their children "try hard." This approach helps to create a positive environment, which generally encourages children to behave well.

Other parents focus more attention on their children's achievements. They praise what their children produce—first words, drawings, correct spelling, reading aloud, good grades at school, success in a sports activity, and so forth. In these situations, too, praise encourages children to continue these successes. Both praising the effort and praising the outcome can be very effective ways to encourage children to achieve and grow.

What few parents practice, however, is positive reinforcement in the context of a deliberate system of discipline. Used in such a framework, positive reinforcement can encourage children to undertake tasks independently, replace undesirable habits with better ones, and behave according to the family's standards every day.

This deliberate use of positive reinforcement in planned and managed discipline techniques is the subject of this chapter and the next. In the very best sense, *these techniques are a practical application of the fundamental principle: parents' attention is their most powerful discipline tool. This chapter focuses on two specific techniques that deliberately and consistently use positive reinforcement as part of a 4-Cs system of clear, consistent, contingent consequences. The first is* Praise for the Expected; *the second,* the Learned Rewards System.

Does using these techniques mean that spontaneous hugs, praise, and treats go out the window? Absolutely not! These always will and should be an important part of loving parenting. Applying these techniques does not exclude other uses of positive reinforcement. Many situations in which parents will want to encourage an achievement or an attitude with attention and positive rewards fall outside of these particular techniques. The techniques provide structured tools that parents can add to their repertoire of discipline options.

The techniques described in this chapter and the next fall within the positive side of discipline. They help to foster desired behaviors. Other techniques, which are described in Chapters 7 and 8, take the reverse approach. They round out the system of discipline by using a combination of techniques to eliminate undesirable behaviors.

Praise for the Expected

When children are generally behaving well, their parents do not need to praise them each time they act as expected. At some point, however, nearly all children behave in inappropriate ways, and sometimes these behaviors become habits. For example, they dawdle getting dressed in the morning or coming to dinner, they fail to pick up their toys when asked to, they put off doing homework, or they whine at the grocery store. Such behaviors frustrate parents and often result in some unpleasant times for the whole family. It is such "bad habits"—patterns of behavior in which children repeatedly fail to comply with specific directions or expectations—that require systematic attention to change.

When children misbehave, parents often respond by repeating their instructions and reminding the children of the expectations. Sometimes these reminders turn into nagging and may even escalate into anger. (Chapter 2 describes why anger is counterproductive or even destructive.) Instead of drawing attention to their children's misdeeds, parents can often turn the children around by focusing their attention on positive alternatives and reinforcing these. Encouraging children's appropriate, compliant behavior in this way is in the children's long-term best interest. The results may also improve parents' peace of mind and household harmony.

Even when a child has formed a bad habit, he may occasionally comply. In such a situation, the parent often reacts by thinking, "Whew! At last he did what he was supposed to!" The natural reaction is to feel relieved, but not delighted. After all, the parent reasons, the child has not demonstrated some great accomplishment or done something wonderful, but has merely obeyed—finally! So even though the child has behaved according to expectations, the parent shows no outward response.

This logic is understandable. By opting not to respond to such moments, however, the parent loses an opportunity to reinforce the preferred behavior. Thus, she also loses a chance to help her child change an undesirable habit. So why not take advantage of such moments?

One way to do so is by employing Praise for the Expected—a specific method that employs positive reinforcement as part of a system of clear, consistent, contingent consequences. This technique is grounded in behavioral theory whose validity has been borne out through repeated testing in many different situations.

Unlike some other positive reinforcement techniques, Praise for the Expected focuses on abundantly praising specific, predefined behaviors.

Praise for the Expected is the deliberate, specific use of praise to help encourage a child's habit of appropriate behavior, while at the same time minimizing her misbehavior. In order to promote such change, a parent gives a lot of positive attention to his child when she behaves according to specific, defined rules—most of which are normally expected behaviors. In fact, this extraordinary response to ordinary behavior is often necessary to bring about the desired result.

In contrast to Praise for the Expected, what typically happens is that the child receives a lot of attention when she misbehaves. Parents ask, "Why does my child work so hard to get my negative attention, when I am so willing to give her my positive attention?" The fact is that when parent and child are locked in an

AT AGE THREE, Jenny had become something of a holy terror in the grocery store. She begged for treats, grabbed unwanted items from the shelves, opened packages in the cart, and cried loudly or even screamed when she was reprimanded. Her mother grew to dread every trip to the market, because each one meant a confrontation.

I suggested to Mom that she work on changing Jenny's grocery store behavior by praising her effusively when she behaved well and giving her less attention when she misbehaved. Mom was to begin by reminding Jenny before they went into the store that she was counting on Jenny to be on her best behavior—and that this meant she was to touch only the toy she brought with her, and to be pleasant and quiet. Then as they went through the store, Mom was to give Jenny minimal or no attention when she misbehaved, but give her a lot of very specific praise, smiles, and hugs when she did as she was expected. For instance, when Jenny sat quietly in the cart, Mom was to smile and say, "It makes me so proud of you when you sit quietly in the cart like this!"

Mom's first reaction was a natural one: why should she praise Jenny when she was just behaving as she was supposed to? Despite her skepticism, she tried the technique, and within three weeks, they were enjoying their trips to the grocery store together. Jenny had "learned" that good behavior won Mom's positive attention. And Mom had "learned" that setting clear expectations and praising her daughter when she met them produced good results. Mom was giving Jenny Praise for the Expected—and it worked!

angry encounter, the parent is so fully focused on the child that the parent gives her 100 percent of his attention—and it is undivided attention that the child really craves.

The problem, of course, is that the parent's attention—especially in such powerful, although negative, doses—actually reinforces the child's misbehavior and thus increases the likelihood that it will recur. So the question for the parent becomes how to use his attention in a way that helps that pattern to change. The answer lies in giving his child attention primarily in ways that positively reinforce the desirable behavior and thus encourage the child to swap the old habit for a new one.

The Praise for the Expected technique that I recommend using to change such behaviors is based on the 4 Cs: clear, consistent, contingent consequences. It begins with the parent developing a plan. First, *the parent decides which behavior he wants his child to change. He makes very certain that the child understands exactly what is expected of her. Then the parent systematically ensures that every time the child behaves appropriately, she immediately receives praise.* This is a very specific and consistent application of the popular concept of "caught you being good." The goal here is for the parent and all other caregivers to deliberately give the child positive attention (consequences) every time (consistent) she performs the defined behavior correctly (contingent). Conversely, she is to receive less attention when she misbehaves.

Each time the child performs the identified behavior well, the parent lets her know that he is noticing. He gives the child praise and encouragement, smiles and hugs. *The words he uses are carefully chosen to make it clear to the child that she is receiving this positive attention because she has performed the defined behavior in the right way.* The parent may use phrases such as, "I like it when you . . . ," "It makes me very proud of you when you . . . ," or "I'm so happy with you when you . . . ." These expressions make clear the connection between the desired behavior and the parent's approval.

By emphasizing that he is "pleased," "happy," or "delighted" by the child's compliance, the parent is using positive social reinforcement. Such reinforcement automatically increases the likelihood that the child will repeat the desired behavior.

If the parent praises the expected behavior consistently, and continues to make clear the if-then relationship between the child's behavior and the parent's rewarding the child with positive attention, usually the child turns the desirable behavior into a habit. At this point, the parent may discontinue using the system and reinstitute it only when the child slips back into old patterns.

This application of the 4 Cs' use of positive reinforcement in Praise for the Expected makes the technique both remarkably simple and particularly effective. Parents can use it as soon as children are old enough to understand the concept of rules—around age three—and can continue to use it through the teenage years.

Sometimes, however, when parents are trying to get their children to adopt new behaviors, a more highly structured reinforcement system than Praise for the Expected may be needed. Many systems of token reinforcement are being used today. The one I have developed and carefully refined differs from other systems in some important ways.

The Learned Rewards System: The Marble Jar

The Learned Rewards System supplements parents' spontaneous hugs and praise with a well-defined system of token reinforcement. This model of positive reinforcement might be considered an "engineering" approach to establishing desired habits. It is designed to help children learn new tasks or encourage them to become more consistent and independent in performing chores they already know how to do. Parents usually can use this system with children from ages three to about twelve.

Use the Learned Rewards System to help a child focus on doing certain daily chores in a clearly defined way every time. At the same time that he learns to do his chores correctly, he also learns the if-then relationship between doing work and earning rewards—the foundation for an important life lesson.

Here is how it works: Together, parents and child define certain "jobs" for which the child will be responsible each day. Then the parent uses a system of positive reinforcement, rewarding the child with tokens and praise each time he performs a specified job to defined standards. At the end of each day, the child exchanges his tokens for a predetermined amount of time in a play activity.

Although this approach might appear cold or manipulative, it is a very loving and straightforward approach to positive discipline: the child and parent become willing partners in establishing certain desirable behaviors. Immediate positive reinforcement marks their collaboration each time the child performs the behavior, and an incentive is structured to help him focus on performing all the defined behaviors correctly over the course of a day. The child not only "earns" rewards—he also "learns" the relationship between completing his jobs correctly and receiving rewards.

The Learned Rewards System works particularly well as a means of encouraging children to perform tasks independently. Children who are between six and twelve years old often need to improve habits like getting ready for school on time; putting their jackets, books, and lunch boxes away; completing homework; helping with dinner preparations; and getting to bed on time. Younger children, too, respond well to this system. Those who are between four and five years old learn to perform tasks like getting dressed on time, brushing their teeth after meals, and picking up toys.

The Marble Jar is the primary "tool" used in the Learned Rewards System. It is simply a clear jar into which marbles are placed. Marbles (or poker chips or some other tokens) are the physical means used to track the child's success in completing her jobs. The parent and child agree upon a certain few tasks, and they clearly define the standards for successful completion. Each time the child performs one of these behaviors in the correct way, he earns a marble, which the parent places in the Marble Jar. At the end of every day, these tokens are turned in for a predetermined reward of some playtime activity.

Three Essential Questions

The Learned Rewards System is based on a plan the parent creates with the child's involvement. The plan begins with answering these three essential questions:

1. What three to five tasks or behaviors are the most important to focus on now?
2. How are those tasks or behaviors defined? What are the standards—the elements that constitute the right behaviors or ways to perform the tasks?
3. What daily play activity does the child enjoy enough to have as a reward?

The following paragraphs explain these questions more completely.

Which Behaviors? The first question that parents must answer is, "What behaviors or tasks are the most important for the child to learn to perform independently now?" It is important to limit the number of behaviors so that both the child and the parent can focus on them consistently, day after day.

Selecting a small number of chores helps the child to focus on learning to perform them independently. Allowing the child to have a say in deciding which chores are important increases his interest in earning the marbles.

It is equally important to select tasks at which the child has a very high probability of success. A child is most likely to develop good habits and be willing to learn and improve other habits when he experiences frequent and immediate positive reinforcement. Ensuring that he can succeed at his tasks and thus experience this reinforcement is the key to this positive system of discipline.

Which behaviors are "most important" varies from family to family and from child to child. They need to be chores or behaviors that occur every day. Generally, they either help the child become more self-sufficient or encourage him to contribute to the family's household responsibilities, or both. For example, a job for a young child might be to learn how to make her bed; for an older one who already knows how to make his bed, the job might be to make his bed neatly every day on his own. The younger child is becoming more self-sufficient; the older one is assuming a household responsibility.

How Defined? One major reason for using the Learned Rewards System is to decrease the frequency of arguments, so it is very important that the parent and child agree not only on exactly *what the task is* but also on exactly *what constitutes satisfactory performance*. Creating a clear definition establishes a consistent standard. This standard allows both the child and the parent to assess the behavior objectively and determine whether the marble can be awarded.

Together, parents and child set the "standards" for each chore. It is the parent's job to ensure that the child clearly understands not only that she *must* do each chore, but also *how* she must do it.

To establish standards, the parents and child must not only think about the right way to do the job, but also anticipate how it might be done in unacceptable ways. If, for example, the child has a habit of cutting corners or hiding mistakes, it may be important to anticipate these and make clear the differences between the acceptable standards to earn the marble and any other ways of getting the job done. This kind of forethought can help prevent the frustration and confusion that can occur when standards must be reworked.

Although the parent and child agree on these standards, it is up to the parent to ensure that the child understands exactly how she must do each job in order to earn her marble. From the outset, there must be no confusion or discrepancy between the child's and the parent's interpretations of precisely what is expected. The standards they set should include an agreement on the number of reminders the child will be allowed.

Once clear standards are agreed upon and in place, the child usually can determine whether she is performing her task in the way that will allow her to get her marble. She has the information she needs in order to earn her reward, and as a result, she and her parents have fewer arguments.

In contrast to setting clearly defined standards, parents sometimes make statements like "If you are good," or "If you behave

When Jimmy and his parents sat down to talk about his new Marble Jar, they agreed that one of his jobs would be to get himself dressed every morning. A young six-year-old, Jimmy had a habit of dawdling, and he was also easily distracted. So Mom and Dad knew they'd better be very clear about what they meant by "getting dressed."

Mom explained to him that the first part of his job was to wash his hands and face with soap, water, and a washcloth, and then rinse and dry those same places. Then he was to put on all the clothes they had laid out together the night before. Since Jimmy almost always managed to forget his shoes and socks, they made very sure he understood that in order to earn his marble he had to put those on, too. The final part of his "getting dressed" job was to brush his hair.

Unfortunately, they had already established a pattern of reminding Jimmy repeatedly and sending him back to his room to finish dressing. Now they needed to undo that habit, so they agreed that he could have only one reminder in order to earn his marble. If he did not do all the parts of his job, or if they had to remind him more than once, there would be no marble.

Finally, he had to be completely finished getting dressed and at the breakfast table by 7:00 a.m. With such explicit standards, Jimmy knew exactly what he had to do, and soon he was at the table every morning on time—fully dressed.

yourself," as conditions for receiving a reward. Such statements actually confuse children: what conditions constitute "good" in the parent's mind may be very different from those in the child's. Without a clear, specific definition of what behaviors are included in "good" or "behave yourself," the child cannot be certain how she is expected to behave. Such statements leave standards open to interpretation and lead to arguments.

Which Reward Activity? Once the parent and child have clearly identified and defined the jobs, the next step is to identify the most suitable reward activity. They should choose a favorite play activity that the child enjoys every day. This should not be an activity that is important to his development, such as reading or playing with friends. Instead, it should be an activity like watching television or playing computer games, which he enjoys and wants to do every day but which contributes little or nothing to his growth.

The Learned Rewards System turns a play activity into a reward. The child earns playtime, and in doing so learns the if-then relationship between work and play. *If* he does his jobs, *then* he will get to play.

The choice of a normal, daily activity as a reward is one of the significant differences between the Learned Rewards System and many other reward systems currently in use. It may seem strange or even unkind to use a child's playtime as a reward for performing chores. In reality, it is highly effective and children tend to accept it as very reasonable.

The first advantage of using a play activity as a reward is that children really like the play activity. They will work to earn this privilege every single day, so it becomes a powerful incentive for them to complete the assigned tasks consistently. The second advantage of a playtime reward is that it is timely. With this reward, children have the chance to receive their reward during the same day they earned it, every single day. The immediacy of the reward is an important factor in its effectiveness. Third, using a play activity as a reward is easy for a parent to administer. Since playtime is a part of the household routine, it requires no special resources or conditions. This means that it can be used consistently, whereas a more burdensome reward is less likely to be used reliably.

Elements of the System

Once the parent has answered these three questions—which behaviors, how defined, and which reward activities—she has the basic "information" required to create the rewards system.

The system is, deliberately, very simple. The parent begins by deciding on the maximum amount of time she wants to allow the child to spend in the reward activity each day, and then divides the time by the number of tasks the child is to perform. She then knows how much reward time to allow for each marble the child receives.

For example, if the parent wants her child to watch a maximum of one hour of TV per day and decides to focus on four behaviors, then each marble is worth 15 minutes. Under these rules, if the child performed three of his four jobs to acceptable standards, he would earn 45 minutes of TV time. If the parent were comfortable with two hours of reward time, she would make each marble worth one half hour. Table 5.1 illustrates how one family set up their youngest child's Learned Rewards System.

Parents should take care to keep the Learned Rewards System very simple. The number of jobs and related points should be limited to a few, and the standards for each task defined clearly but simply. Sometimes parents and children are tempted to overengi-

Table 5.1 Marble Jar System Example

Jobs	Number of Marbles	Reward Time
1. Get dressed by yourself in the morning.	1	15 minutes
2. Put away all your belongings as soon as you get home from school.	1	15 minutes
3. Set the table for dinner.	1	15 minutes
4. Pick up all your toys before dinner.	1	15 minutes
Total	4	60 minutes

neer their system. It may seem like fun to create intricate rules, regulations, and conditions for points. If the Learned Rewards System becomes too complex, however, parents and children soon feel that it requires too much effort, and they abandon it.

Why It Works

When the system is well designed and clearly explained it is almost always immediately successful. There are two reasons for its effectiveness. First, most children find getting the marble to be highly rewarding. The marble itself is a tangible reminder that the child has behaved well. Moreover, since the parent *always* pairs the act of giving the marble with praising the child, earning a marble always results in both tangible and social reinforcement for the desired behavior. So in and of itself, the act of awarding the marble helps increase the likelihood that the child will do her jobs.

The Learned Rewards System reinforces a child twice. First, she receives both a marble and praise as soon as she completes each chore. Then, at the end of every day, her behavior is reinforced again when she receives her earned playtime in the Marble Jar ritual.

Second, most children are highly motivated to earn television, computer, or video-game time. They are accustomed to watching TV shows to the very end and playing games until their conclusion. Thus if, on a given day, a child earns only enough marbles to watch three-quarters of a program (i.e., he does not have enough marbles to "purchase" time to watch the ending), then he has an incentive to change his behavior. Usually, when a child has not gotten all his reward time on one day, he tries very hard to earn all his marbles on the next. He becomes motivated to do all his tasks correctly so that he can watch the entire program or play his game for the full amount of time.

Introducing the System

Since the Learned Rewards System is based on managing behavior through clear, consistent, contingent consequences, it works only if the child understands exactly how the new system operates and what is expected of her. One of the factors in the system's effectiveness is introducing it in the appropriate context. Before beginning to use the Learned Rewards System, the parents explain it to the child in a calm, quiet, and loving manner. The time to do this is not when the child has just misbehaved, but rather when both she and the parent are calm and happy, and when they have plenty of time to talk it through.

When parents introduce the Learned Rewards System, they begin by explaining to the child that they want her to learn to do certain "jobs" very well all the time, and that to do this, they have a new system—the Marble Jar. They tell her that although she does most of her jobs well some of the time, she needs to turn these into every-time habits. They explain that the Marble Jar will help her remember to do her jobs the right way all the time, and that she will earn her playtime by doing her jobs well. Calling the child's tasks, chores, and behaviors, "jobs" may help her under-

JACK WAS A good-natured boy, but like most children, sometimes he did not do what was expected of him. At seven, he had abundant energy, which he needed to burn off. In his eagerness to play outside, he would rush home from school, drop his belongings in the middle of the floor, and run outside in his school clothes. In fact, this became something of a habit and caused frequent confrontations with his parents. There were other chores, too, that he often forgot to do.

His parents decided to try the Marble Jar with him. They explained the new system to him and asked which of his "jobs" he thought he most needed to improve. Not surprisingly, he picked several that were subjects of confrontation. He also chose cleaning his room. Although his parents had not made an issue of Jack's messiness in his own space, it turned out that he often felt frustrated because he could not find certain belongings, and sometimes he even broke some treasured toys by stepping on them.

After discussing the possible jobs for Jack to work on, they all agreed on four. Jack wanted picking up the toys in his room on the list, and he agreed to his parents' request to put his books and school clothes away every day. Together they agreed to focus on a list of behaviors that included what each deemed most important.

stand the general principle that work must be completed before the rewards of play or free time are granted in society. In fact, the parent may make the analogy: the child will earn her TV time just as Daddy and Mommy earn theirs—by finishing the required jobs for the day.

The parents then ask the child which jobs she thinks she most needs to work on. In many years of experience, I have found that children usually have a fairly clear understanding of what they are supposed to do every day. Allowing them from the beginning to help select which behaviors to work on gives them a real sense of ownership. They are more likely to follow through, and being given this responsibility encourages them to accept others.

Once they agree on the daily Marble Jar jobs, the parents and child work together to define the standards for them. It is important for the child to participate in this process, because it is part of the learning involved. Through the process of setting standards, she begins to understand that doing a job involves not only getting it done, but also getting it done well. Since learning to do such jobs independently is a key goal of the Learned Rewards System, it is important for parents and child to agree on the number of reminders the child may have for each job. I recommend that it usually be no more than two. Letting the child have more than two reminders defeats two fundamental purposes of the Learned Rewards System: (1) to encourage the child to accept responsibility, and (2) to help her become more independent.

Ensuring that the child understands exactly what constitutes the correct performance of the targeted behavior—and what does not—not only helps the child to do her jobs correctly, but also helps to prevent arguments about whether or not a marble has been earned.

After the parents and child decide on the jobs, they create a list of them as a visual reminder the child can use every day. This can be a written list for an older child or pictures for one who does not read yet. The list should be placed on the refrigerator or a bulletin board where the child can see it every day.

The parents explain that each time the child completes the entire job the right way, they will immediately put a marble in her Marble Jar, and each marble will earn her a certain number of minutes of reward time. When first setting up this system, the parents show the child the actual jar and marbles. While it might be tempting to allow the child to drop her own marble into the jar, it is best for a parent to do so. Not only does this provide the parent with a perfect opportunity to reinforce the good behavior with praise, but keeping control of the jar also prevents the child from awarding herself a marble when the standards have not been met or when she mischievously decides to slip one in.

Finally, the parents set a specified time toward the end of the day when they will count the marbles in the jar together. The number of marbles will tell them how many minutes of reward time she has earned.

Using the System

Once the parents are certain that the child understands both how he is expected to perform his jobs and how the system will work, they begin to use the Marble Jar consistently, day after day. *It is important that the child always experiences the system in the same way, no matter who is in charge.* Since the jobs for which the Learned Rewards System work best are usually centered in the home, it is critical that both parents not only use the system consistently, but also get the complete cooperation of all caregivers. They need to explain the system as thoroughly to the child's other caregivers as they have to the child himself, and then ensure that it is always used as specified.

Awarding the marble should always occur immediately after the child has completed a task. The parent can make the most of this opportunity with smiles, hugs, and praise. By recounting specific elements of the job that the child has done well—particularly if these aspects of the task have been difficult for him—and letting him know that his success makes her proud and happy, she further reinforces his behavior, thus increasing the likelihood that he will repeat it.

If the child fails to complete the job, or does not meet the defined standards, the parent plainly states that he did not earn the marble and, if necessary, briefly reminds the child of the reason. Unless the child genuinely does not understand where he has failed, the parent immediately ends the discussion. If, instead, the parent were to prolong it by negotiating new conditions, providing lengthy explanations, or arguing about why the marble was not awarded, she would defeat the purpose of the Learned Rewards System. Giving attention to the child for failing to successfully perform his task actually reinforces his mistakes.

Since the Marble Jar becomes the authority, parents and child no longer argue over reward time. The result: less conflict.

Opening the Marble Jar every day becomes a family ritual, and it provides yet another opportunity to reinforce the child's success with praise. Soon after they initiate the Learned Rewards System, parents usually discover that the child begins to perceive the Marble Jar as the authority, and in fact, the system works best when this happens. Parents can even encourage this notion. With a young child, the parent may make a game of asking the jar how many marbles it has. It may seem illogical or even downright silly to adults, but in the child's eyes, the jar takes on a life of its own. It is the jar, and not her parent, that "tells" her how much reward time she has earned—or how much she is *not* going to get. If there are only one or two marbles in the jar, the child can literally see that she has earned less than the full amount of her TV time.

One of the great advantages of the Marble Jar is that it greatly helps reduce arguments about privileges. The system largely takes Mom and Dad out of the equation, and it is very hard for even the most irascible child to argue very long with a jar! Ultimately, through this objective system, the child learns that her marbles—and hence her rewards—are a direct consequence of her own successful accomplishments.

Once the child begins to adopt and perform a job consistently, she and her parents may agree to eliminate it from the list and substitute another. Of course, the time does come when the Marble Jar is no longer needed. Parents may choose to stop using it and then reinstitute it if behaviors crop up that might benefit from this kind of focused and systematic attention. The Marble Jar is simply a tool, and like all tools, the user determines whether it is needed or not.

The Marble Jar often produces a highly beneficial side effect. Many parents find that, in addition to serving as a useful and effective tool, the Marble Jar system also causes the parents to become more perceptive, focused, and structured in their daily parenting. Just as the Marble Jar helps children to change certain defined behaviors, it often also helps parents to refine their own expectations, improve the clarity and completeness of their communication with their children, provide positive reinforcement at the right moments, and practice consistency in discipline throughout every day.

Who would have imagined that a few simple marbles and an ordinary little jar could have so much power!

6

"Why Can't I Just Give Him a Toy?" and Other Questions Parents Ask About the Learned Rewards System

> When my daughter is good, I like to reward her
> with a treat. My husband says that's bribery and
> spoiling her. I can see his point, but my parents
> always rewarded me with things I wanted, and I'm
> not spoiled!

Just as there are many different approaches to discipline, there are many opinions about rewards. Different people have experienced different reward systems, so the number of strong opinions on the subject is understandable. Equally understandable is how bewildering it can be to choose the best rewards!

Chapter 5 described two systems of positive reinforcement that I have found highly effective. Inevitably, however, parents have questions about rewards and other aspects of these systems—particularly the Learned Rewards System. This chapter addresses some of the most frequently asked questions.

What's Wrong with Using Tangible Items and Special Treats for Rewards?

The problem with using tangible rewards and many other types of treats is that such rewards tend to be all-or-nothing. So even if a child performs some portion of his tasks well, he does not receive a reward—because he has not done everything on the list. Then his failure to complete all of his tasks overrides his success at a few, and his good deeds go unreinforced.

Many years ago, I did a lot of work with token reward systems. As I worked with parents over time, I realized that many of the systems we set up were not very effective. The problems fell into three categories, all related to aspects of the rewards themselves. The rewards failed to work well because they were based on an interest that proved to be too short-lived, they were too distant in time, or they were too impractical.

Short-Lived Rewards

Often when parents set up a reward system, they choose tangible rewards that they think their children really want and are willing to work for. Understandably, they choose treats in which their children express strong interest. For example, they might choose to reward the performance of a job with baseball cards, new doll clothes, small toys, an ice cream cone, or, as in Jocelyn's case, nail polish.

Tangible rewards usually work once or twice, and sometimes even a few more times. But one main problem is that at some point, the child's interest in the reward wears off, and as it does, so does the incentive to earn it. Then parents begin to hear their children say things like, "I already have enough stickers. I don't need any more," or "There aren't any more Barbie clothes I really like," or "I don't want to go to the playground again. It's boring."

AT AGE TEN, JOCELYN decided that she really hated cleaning her room. Her mother found that getting Jocelyn to uncover the floor—let alone run the vacuum cleaner—took almost the same amount of energy as required to move heaven and earth.

However, Jocelyn had recently discovered nail polish, and she loved trying out every imaginable color. "Aha!" thought her mother, "Here's the solution." She got Jocelyn to agree to clean her room once a week by promising her a new bottle of nail polish each time she completed the task.

The system worked beautifully for about four weeks— then the room started to take on its old messy look again. Why? Jocelyn's passion for nail polish turned out to be fleeting, while her aversion to cleaning remained strong and enduring. So Jocelyn's mother was left with the problem of finding a new incentive as her daughter lost interest in each one.

Thus, the use of such rewards seldom remains effective over a long period time.

If a child loses interest in one reward, why not just switch to another? Of course, it is possible to make a change, and this happens from time to time with playtime rewards, too. But from the outset, it is best to establish a reward that will not need to be renegotiated very often. After all, children's interests can change instantly and often. The toy that is "my very best, most absolute favorite" today may, by tomorrow, be replaced with another, entirely different "absolute favorite."

If the parent frequently has to change rewards to accommodate these changing desires, the focus of the discipline system soon shifts to the reward itself rather than where it belongs: on the child's successful accomplishments. In addition, changing rewards opens the door for wheedling and arguments. So all in all, tangible rewards are generally not very effective tools for reinforcing jobs that parents want the child to make routine.

Time-Delayed Rewards

Another problem that sometimes occurs is having rewards that are too distant in time (i.e, too far removed from the child's completion of her daily jobs) to effectively reinforce them. Like Miguel's parents, many people set up a weekly reward system, with the child earning a checkmark or a sticker for performing each chore. By accumulating a set number of these, the child earns a reward at the end of the week.

One problem is that during the first half of the week, the weekend seems very far off to the child. Thus, the reward does not seem real—certainly not real enough to focus on the day's chores. In such situations, the incentive does not motivate the child to complete her daily chores.

Another failure of such a reward structure is that unless the child performs her tasks correctly for the *entire* week, the child receives no reinforcement at all for any of the times that she performed the tasks correctly. When the objective of a reward system is to reinforce particular behaviors and thereby encourage their repetition, rewards that are delayed too long do not work.

Impractical Rewards

The third type of problem that occurs is choosing rewards that are impractical and thus too uncertain to be effective. Often such rewards depend on external factors that are beyond the child's or even the parent's control.

ON THE DAYS when Miguel felt happy and energetic, he did his chores with scarcely a word. For each one he finished, he got a sticker on his chart. On Saturday, if he had received all his stickers, his parents would give him a dollar. His parents liked the system because it taught him about getting paid for work.

Sometimes, however, Miguel did not get his dollar. He usually did his jobs perfectly on Monday, Tuesday, and even Wednesday. By Thursday, he was tired—a factor that influenced his doing chores that day and sometimes the next. So Saturday was an unhappy day for everyone as Miguel and his parents argued over his lapses late in the week. As the weeks went by, Miguel became less and less interested in doing his chores.

The problem was that the reward was too far removed from Miguel's performing his chores. He did not receive the immediate reinforcement he needed at the moment he finished them, nor was he even rewarded on the same day. When Miguel and his parents switched to the Marble Jar, he soon was performing his chores more eagerly every day. And without arguments, all their days were much happier.

Many parents begin with a good idea, such as making a reward of a parent-child activity: taking a trip to the zoo, going on a bike ride, or playing a game. While such rewards sound ideal for many reasons, in practice they often fail to work. Sometimes the parent's schedule makes it difficult to arrange these activities. Sometimes other factors intervene. Even though these may include legitimate conflicts such as another child's baseball game or ballet lesson, or contrary conditions like illness or miserable weather, the result is that the reward activity is postponed or cancelled. No matter how justifiable the reason, the effect is the same: missing rewards cannot reinforce the desired behavior.

Of course, all of the preceding rewards can have their place in the total scheme of parenting. Occasional celebratory gifts or treats when a child has accomplished something important can be wonderful reinforcements. Also, it is important for families to enjoy pleasurable outings and educational experiences together. All such rewards are valuable and can be very reinforcing; however, they are not useful in context of the Learned Rewards System.

Isn't It Unfair to Use a Child's Playtime as a Reward?

Having determined that rewards that are too short-lived, too distant in time, or too impractical usually fail to be effective rewards for daily chores, I began to search for a different kind of reward system. I thought about what might inspire children to perform tasks every single day, and that led me to ask what children most enjoy doing every day. At that point I began to consider how playtime might be structured as a reward.

My initial reaction—much like that of many parents—was that it seemed unfair to make children earn playtime. After all, playtime is a normal and even important part of childhood. In the "real" (adult) world, however, people must do their work before they earn their pleasure. I realized that helping children learn this if-then concept of "responsibility before reward" early in life would be helpful to them in the long term. Thus, the notion of "earned rewards" became the basis for my Learned Rewards System. This system is designed not only as a discipline technique, but also as a learning process in which children grow to understand the connection between responsible behavior and rewards.

I also wanted to ensure, however, that in structuring playtime as a reward, parents never deprived their children of important learning activities. Therefore, I do not recommend that parents use playing with friends, reading books, special instruction (such as music or horseback-riding lessons), or playing sports as Learned Rewards, because these activities are very important to children's growth and development.

The reward activities that I do recommend to parents are ones that children enjoy but that do not add any significant value to their lives. Top on the list of such activities are watching television and playing electronic games. Although television can be educational, most of what children watch makes little difference in their lives. The same is true for purely recreational computer and video games (not educational ones). Despite what most people think, research has demonstrated that devices like video games do not aid children's thinking, enhance eye-hand coordination, or build concentration skills.

What if My Child Does Not Like Television or Electronic Games?

Some children have escaped the lure of electronic entertainment and do not like to watch television or play computer games enough for these to serve as daily incentives. In such situations, parents need to think about how their child spends his time. What activities does he engage in every day?

In choosing among these, parents should select one that their child wants to do every day, and that he would miss if he could not do it. They should also consider whether limiting his time at this activity to only what he earned or failing to earn time at this activity altogether would deprive the child of an important experience. Activities that have proven to be effective rewards for some children are playing with a doll or toy car collection, doing art projects, and building models. In each of these cases, the child was permitted to earn reward time in an activity that he was already engaged in every day, and in which he had been interested for a very long time. With the art and model projects, the parents had to take responsibility for providing the appropriate supplies. Apart from that, all of these were activities that the child could perform completely on his own, and they served as excellent incentives for the child to do his jobs well every day.

What if I *Need* My Child to Spend Time in Front of the TV?

While many parents deliberately limit the amount of time their children watch TV, some use the TV as a babysitter in order to have some quiet time of their own every day. They may want the children out from underfoot while they shower and dress in the morning or when they prepare dinner at the end of the day, and parking the kids in front of the TV at those times works well for them. A small number of parents find that in order to meet their own needs, they use the TV to distract the children for a large portion of the day.

In such cases, the parents generally need to think a little differently about reward time in the Learned Rewards System. Since each family situation is different, no single best solution fits all of them. Parents can generally solve the problem, however, and they may find that it still works to turn TV time into reward time.

One solution that has worked for some families is for the parents to determine exactly how much time their children spend watching television every day, and then divide the total by the number of chores. For example, instead of each chore being worth fifteen minutes, for these families each marble might be worth an hour. Children in these families are so accustomed to watching TV that they are motivated to continue doing so, and they will work to earn their TV time. Usually they miss doing chores only one or two days at the beginning before settling into a pattern of getting their jobs done and earning their TV time; so the parents experience only a short period of disruption.

Parents who use the TV as a babysitter at particular times of day but are otherwise comfortable restricting their children's television consumption can also adapt the Learned Rewards System to suit their lifestyle. In these cases, the child's TV reward times must occur outside of those scheduled for the parents' convenience. This reward system usually does not work quite as well as one in which the child can watch TV only during the time that she earns. In most cases, however, if the child clearly understands the system, it works well enough to motivate her.

In households where the TV is left on for much of the day, families may have to cross television off the list of possible rewards. Instead, they may choose other effective rewards, including video-game time and other play activities such as those mentioned earlier.

Some parents find that setting up a structured reward system causes them to assess for the first time exactly how much TV their children actually watch. Sometimes, when they total it all up, they are shocked by the large percentage of waking, free time their children spend in front of the TV. When they consider its potential impact, they sometimes realign their priorities and consciously choose to restrict television time, difficult as that sometimes can be.

Whether or not they choose to continue allowing their children to watch lengthy amounts of TV, parents discover that when they employ a more structured approach to discipline, their children begin to behave better. With calmer children, the parents generally find that they do not need to use the TV as a babysitter quite so much of the time.

Can I Permit My Child to Earn Extra Marbles?

In general, I discourage this "extra credit" practice for two reasons. First, adding this element makes the system more confusing. The Learned Rewards System is intended to fit easily into both the parents' and the child's daily routines. Adding extra jobs and marbles means more for both the parent and the child to pay attention to. Second, allowing a child to earn extra marbles dilutes his focus on the assigned jobs. If the child is eagerly trying to earn extra marbles or make up for marbles he has failed to earn, then he is not learning to do his daily jobs consistently.

Having said that, I don't think harm is done if a child is allowed to earn extra marbles *occasionally*—preferably on a weekend. *Occasionally* is the operative word here. In making this decision, parents need to consider several factors. One is whether the child is making progress and maintaining some consistency in his daily jobs. If he is, then letting him earn extra marbles may further encourage his sense of responsibility. If he is not, then the extra chores will detract from the purpose. A second factor is the parents' willingness to allow the child extra time in the play activity. If they are comfortable with letting him occasionally sit in front of the TV or computer game for more than the usual allotted time limit, then allowing him to earn that extra time is acceptable. If they are not, then they may want to leave their

Learned Rewards program as is and find other ways to encourage his initiative.

How Do I Manage Computer Games and Other Rewards That Do Not Run on a Fixed Schedule?

Television is easy to use as a reward because programs are scheduled for fixed amounts of time. Electronic games are not quite so easy, because they are designed to entice the player to finish a game, and many are not time-based. If a parent and child agree to use computer games or other rewards in which the completion of the activity is not determined by a preset amount of time, it is important to talk about this together when setting up the reward system.

One solution is to determine the amount of time it usually takes for the child to play her favorite game, and then make each marble worth a specific number of games. This means that the amount of reward time will vary slightly from one day to the next. Another solution for games of short duration is to establish a time frame, with the understanding that when the time is up, the child will be allowed to complete her current game but not start another one.

What if I Want to Reward Bedtime Behaviors?

Having a child prepare for and get to bed on time are issues many parents face. Making these into jobs in the Learned Rewards System can help the child to accomplish them consistently, and it is certainly possible to structure the reward time to achieve these goals.

For bedtime responsibilities, the marble should be awarded at night before the child goes to sleep. The parents can set up the system so that the child can turn in his marble for reward time either early the next morning or later the next day. Morning reward time is more effective, if it is possible to schedule it then. If the marble is to be swapped for time later in the day, the parents will be most successful in reinforcing the bedtime behavior if they remind their child soon after he wakes that he earned his marble the night before. This gives them another opportunity to praise him for doing his bedtime job well.

How Do I Switch My Child's Jobs?

The Learned Rewards System makes it easy for parents to help their children continue to become more proficient and independent by taking on new jobs as they master old ones. A child has mastered a job if she performs it very consistently, day after day, with no reminders at all.

Parents should keep a job on the list and continue to give rewards until it is clear that the child has mastered the job. Then they can take that job off the list and replace it with another. When talking about making the change, the parent can take another opportunity to celebrate the fact that the child has done this job so well every day without reminders. At the same time, the parent must make very clear that the child is to continue doing this job, even though it is not on the Marble Jar list. Since the child has made this job into a habit, she usually is both willing and able to continue doing it.

Children usually have no difficulty understanding the concept of switching jobs on the list. Once they have mastered a task, they are usually ready to move on to a new one, especially when they participate in choosing it.

How Do I Manage the Rewards with More Than One Child?

The mechanics of the system are easy to administer. The parents use a separate jar and list of tasks for each child. Even if one child needs the structure of the Learned Rewards System much more than his siblings, the system is most effective if all children in a family have the same structure. Otherwise, the child who is singled out feels as though he is being punished—and punishment is contrary to this system's purpose of encouraging desirable behaviors through positive reinforcement.

Managing the reward time sometimes requires careful forethought. Electronic games are the easiest to administer. If each child plays alone, then it is a matter of arranging the schedules so that each can have the full amount of his time without interruption. If two siblings play these games together, each is allowed to play only his earned amount of time. If one child must stop playing before the other, then the child who has earned more time may continue to play solitary games after the other has finished. If one child regularly earns more time than the other, the contrast generally provides an incentive for the less diligent child.

Television reward time can be a little trickier to manage, but the same principles apply. If there are several children in the family, Learned Rewards are easiest to manage when the children all watch the same programs together. Then if one child has earned less time than the others have, that child must leave the room where the TV is located and go to another activity immediately when his time is up. This causes some displeasure, but if the siblings get to continue watching TV, the child will be more interested in earning all of his TV time the next day.

If the children cannot agree on programs they all want to watch, then each chooses a time period when he has control over what program is watched. In households where there is more than one television, then each child can use his reward time to watch his favorite programs.

Can I Use Different Rewards to Promote Other Behaviors at the Same Time I Am Using the Learned Rewards System?

As long as the parents and children are able to maintain focus on the selected Marble Jar jobs, it can be effective to encourage other behaviors with other types of rewards. Of course, other reward systems also may be useful at times when the family is not using the Learned Rewards System.

Using other types of rewards can be helpful in several situations. One example of such a situation is bedtime. Many parents want to structure bedtime routines that encourage their children to get to bed on time. One such structure requires a child to complete her bedtime preparations at a certain time with only one reminder. When she accomplishes this, she is rewarded with extra reading time before bed. Although in most situations I discourage parents from using reading as a reward, in this case, allowing extra reading does not limit any of the child's other reading time during the day. Also, reading is a calm, soothing activity that helps many children go to sleep.

Another example of a situation that can benefit from another reward structure is the family dinner. Some parents like to encourage their children to sit pleasantly at the dinner table until everyone is finished, and then ask to be excused before leaving. For a child who is restless and resists sitting still, a structured incentive may encourage him to behave appropriately. In this case, being allowed to have dessert might be a fitting reward for following the dinnertime rules. Of course, this would work only if the parent were comfortable letting the child have dessert every day.

Can I Use the Learned Rewards System to Change Any Behavior at All?

The Learned Reward System is a technique specifically structured to encourage children to take responsibility for performing daily tasks. Appropriate jobs include doing homework, emptying the trash, putting away coats and boots immediately when coming inside, and other such habitual activities that a child must learn to master independently. In contrast, the Learned Rewards System is not intended to change some other types of behavior, particularly those that are dangerous, aggressive, or infrequent. Some alternative discipline techniques are outlined in the following sections.

Dangerous Behaviors

When a child does something that could hurt himself or someone else—touching a hot stove, running into the street, or playing with knives—parents need to intervene immediately and try to make a lasting impression. The first order of business is to prevent harm; the second is to try to teach the child not to repeat the behavior. This is the only situation in which I recommend using a loud, emphatic voice. The point here is for the parent to do something so dramatic and behave in a way that is so different from his norm, that the child remembers it and does not repeat the behavior.

Aggressive Behaviors

The Learned Rewards System is not the right tool to address aggressive behaviors—refusing to obey a direct order, hitting, throwing tantrums, behaving rudely, and other angry outbursts. The whole range of negative behaviors is best handled through the No Reply and Cool Down Techniques, which will be explained in the next chapter. Trying to use the Learned Rewards System to modify aggressive behaviors would result in a confusing and misleading tangle of negatives: it would reward a child for *not* behaving in ways he is *not* supposed to. The Learned Rewards System is designed to reinforce desirable behaviors, not to reward the lack of bad behavior.

Infrequent Issues

This discipline technique also is not designed to deal with infrequent issues—an occasional deviation from the agreed-upon route home from school, or an uncharacteristically careless treatment of a homework assignment. Occasional deviations from the rules or from expected behaviors can be handled with a brief conversation. The fact that the behavior is unusual generally means the parent should not give it a lot of attention. In most cases, it is sufficient and appropriate for the parent to remind the child of the rule and to restate her expectation that the child will follow it in the future. She can further encourage his compliance by praising what he does well most of the time and inspiring him to hold to his usual high standards. Making too much of such occasions is usually not a good idea, because that excess of attention reinforces the misbehavior.

Can I Take Marbles Away if My Child Does Something Wrong During the Day?

In two simple words, *No. Never.* The Learned Rewards System is designed to encourage repetition of desirable behaviors through consistent reinforcement. It is a system of reward, not a system of punishment. Taking away a marble would be a punishment. As such, it could cause a negative reaction, which would completely undermine the positive structure of this discipline technique.

If it is necessary to discipline a child for misbehaving during the same period that the family is using the Learned Rewards System, it is important to separate that situation from the reinforcement she is receiving for having performed her jobs well. The child must clearly understand when her parents are happy with her performance, and she must realize that she is receiving the reward because she has earned it. She must also understand how she has misbehaved and that she will face consequences for that.

How Can I Avoid Making Mistakes That Might Undermine the Learned Rewards System?

The Learned Rewards System is reasonably foolproof. The benefit of using time in a pleasurable activity as a reward is that the child always receives some reinforcement for what he has done well. The child receives instant reinforcement with a marble and praise when he completes his job. Then if he has performed even one of his behaviors well, he also earns some time in a play activity that same day. If the system is structured to use an activity he likes as a reward, then he has an incentive to earn all of his Marble Jar time.

One of the best ways to ensure the success of the Learned Rewards System is to invest time and thought at the outset—that is, while setting up the system. In planning it, parents need to make choices with which they will be completely comfortable over the long term. This is most easily achieved if the parents try to anticipate in advance where the system might go awry, and then take measures to preclude any potential problems right from the beginning.

The biggest risk of failure occurs from lack of consistency. The Learned Rewards System does not require an inordinate amount of parents' time, but parents cannot effectively reinforce the desired behaviors if the system gets lost in the daily shuffle. Structure is important in helping children learn how to behave, and this tool provides a purposeful structure.

Otherwise, parents can prevent difficulties by thinking through the details of administering the system before they start to use it. For some parents, one of the most important factors is controlling the rewards. For example, they may want to strictly limit the amount of time their children spend in front of an electronic screen. This is a very manageable situation. Parents need to set up and explain the system so that even as jobs change, the amount of time in front of the screen can never exceed the limit.

Preventing children from watching TV shows the parents disapprove of is another important issue for many parents. Usually, these parents have made the limits very clear at an earlier time. In setting up the Learned Rewards System, it is important to clarify at the beginning that earned TV time still comes with restrictions, and that the parents still must approve of any program the child watches.

Another issue that occasionally arises is when the Marble Jar is not opened until very late in the day. Then the parent is faced with either denying the child his reward time that day or allowing him to stay up past his bedtime. Setting a fixed window of time for opening the jar and then adhering to it easily solves this problem.

One other sticking point is failing to limit the number of reminders a child may have for any particular task. Without such a limit, reminders may become all too frequent and habitual. In essence, these become nagging, which is unpleasant and, more important, ineffective. Nagging becomes a way of life, and after a while, children dismiss it as a negative personality trait—"My mom is just grouchy!"—rather than see it as a help in changing behavior.

Usually, parents develop sound plans and are able to work out creative alternatives to whatever issues arise over the course of using the Learned Rewards System. Even though consistency is important, nothing about this system must be so rigid that it cannot be changed when necessary. Clear communication is important at these times.

Are There Times When the Learned Rewards System Doesn't Work?

Children are usually very motivated to earn all of their reward time. When they must stop watching TV before the end of a show, or when they do not get to spend as much time playing computer games as they want to, they have a real incentive to earn all of their marbles the next day.

Occasionally, parents find that their child is consistently not earning a marble for a particular job. In this case, the parents need to try to get to the root of why this is happening. Is the job too complex? If so, it can be broken into smaller steps, and then the parents assign only those steps that the child can perform. Is there something about this job that the child feels is unfair or she just hates for some reason? In such situations, parents need to try to understand the problem. Often the child can tell the parent what is bothering her; then they usually can find a solution. In any case, it is very important that the system be set up in such a way that the child can succeed at each task.

Occasionally, a young child around age three is not ready to use the Learned Rewards System. This is clearly the case if the child cannot perform her jobs even when they are broken into very simple steps. Usually this is a matter of not being developmentally ready. In such a case, the parents should just stop using the system and wait until the child is ready before reintroducing it.

For most parents and children, however, the Learned Rewards System works like a charm. The child is motivated to become more independent and responsible, and enjoys earning the reward time. The parents find the system easy to manage and have the pleasure of watching their child grow in positive ways. These can be very happy and productive times. Enjoy them!

7

No Reply and Cool Down: Discipline Techniques That Teach Children How to Manage Their Own Behavior

> After I put her in Time-Out, she keeps yelling. I keep telling her to be quiet, that she's in Time-Out for a reason. But she just keeps on, and we always get into an argument. Time-Out just doesn't work for us.

Whereas Praise for the Expected and the Learned Rewards System are designed to increase the repetition of desirable behaviors, No Reply and Cool Down are focused on eliminating unwanted behaviors. All four techniques are specific ways parents can use their most powerful discipline tool—their own attention—to influence their children's behavior.

Cool Down is a significant modification of Time-Out, a widely used technique with many differing versions. Cool Down is a structured discipline tool designed to help children learn to manage their own behavior—particularly to bring an end to unwanted actions. No Reply is a simple means of extinguishing unwanted behaviors by deliberately ignoring them in a structured process.

Using No Reply

No Reply applies the behavioral principle of extinction in its purest form. The No Reply discipline technique is a simple, clear, structured way of extinguishing unwanted behaviors by ignoring them. It can be used with children from age two through adult.

This technique is most effective in situations when a child tries to get his parents' attention in unpleasant ways—pouting, whining, whimpering, or begging. He usually knows he is not behaving as he ought to. Sometimes he is tired or cranky. Nevertheless, he is capable of better behavior than he is using. Note, however, that No Reply is not suited to dealing with behaviors that cannot or should not be ignored, such as any kind of aggression or dangerous behavior.

The key to No Reply is making sure the child understands the if-then relationship between her behavior and her parents' lack of attention to it. The parent needs to tell her directly that he is going to ignore her because she is not behaving well, and that he will continue to ignore her as long as she persists in this behavior. It is helpful for the parent to use statements such as, "As long as you keep on whining, I will not pay any attention to you," or "You know better than to use that tone of voice. As long as you continue to use it, I will not answer you."

Immediately following such a statement, the parent follows through. By shifting his attention to something or someone else, turning his back toward her, or leaving the room, the parent further communicates that he has withdrawn his attention. Then the parent follows through on his promise to ignore the unwanted

BRITTANY WAS A habitual whiner. Every time she wanted something, she whined to get it. She whined when she wanted to go outside, when she couldn't find her shoes, when she wanted a glass of juice, and when she wanted a treat at the grocery store.

Her mother had a habit, too. Her habit was to respond to Brittany. She told her that whining was unpleasant, that it turned her face into a frown, and that people did not like to be around her when she whined. She told her to stop whining. But Mom never stopped talking to Brittany when she whined. Instead, she kept on paying attention to her whining.

One day, Mom tried a new approach. When Brittany whined, Mom said calmly but firmly, "Brittany, you are to stop whining now. I will not pay any attention to you until you use a pleasant tone of voice." Then she resumed reading her recipe and began cooking.

For the next few minutes, Brittany continued to whine. Then she stopped, peeked around her mother's apron, and said, "Mom, I'm sorry." Her mother smiled, and said, "This is much nicer."

Over the next few days, Brittany still whined sometimes. After all, it was a long-standing habit. Each time, her mother told Brittany that she would ignore her until Brittany changed her tone. Brittany abandoned her whiny voice within two weeks. Mom was astonished, but delighted.

behavior and refuses to take part in further interaction, discussion, or argument. All of this is handled in a very calm manner without anger.

Once the child behaves appropriately, the parent may choose to reinforce the desirable behavior by once again pleasantly giving the child his attention. He may even signal his approval with a brief comment such as "That's better," and a smile.

The following three factors influence the success of No Reply, and each differs from the typical ways many parents handle minor misbehavior. First, the parents must explain to the child the consequences of her misbehavior: being ignored. Second, they stay the course and refuse to give any attention to the child until her behavior improves. Third, the parents remain calm.

Children may or may not immediately stop the behavior the first time No Reply is used. Many parents find, however, that they need to use No Reply only a very few times before the child breaks a particular unpleasant habit.

Using Cool Down to Prevent Meltdowns

When parents first learn the Cool Down technique, they invariably shake their heads and proclaim, "This will never work." Their skepticism usually stems from their previous attempts to use Time-Out, which have not proven successful. To their own astonishment, however, not only does Cool Down work, but also it usually works quickly. Inevitably, they call back to report, "I can't believe it! Cool Down is really working, and it's so much more peaceful at our house!"

The typical pattern of behavior that can be corrected through the use of Cool Down goes something like this: the child misbehaves and when corrected, becomes defiant—arguing and sometimes acting out. The situation escalates from there. A battle ensues, in which the child—and sometimes also the parent—becomes increasingly angry. The example of Jillian and her mother is repeated many times over, in many households.

Unless the cycle is broken, the child does not learn how to manage his own behavior. He learns neither to follow instructions, nor to control his anger. With children over the age of

JILLIAN'S PARENTS WERE enormously frustrated with her. She hated doing chores and frequently responded to their instructions with anger and defiance. "At age seven, she ought to be better behaved," her parents reasoned.

One Saturday, it began as usual. Jillian walked away from the breakfast table without clearing her dishes. When her mother prompted her, she ignored her and kept on going. "Jillian Ann," her mother said, the tension already rising in her voice, "come back here right now and take your dishes to the sink."

"I'll do it later," Jillian said sullenly and left the room. Her mother raised her voice. "Jillian, I said to come back here and clear off these dishes. Now I mean it. Get back here this instant."

Jillian shouted back, "Why do I have to do everything right now? I have a life, too, you know. You're always so mean to me."

At this point her mother began yelling, "You always behave like such a brat. I do everything for you, but you never do anything when I ask you to."

Sadly, if such a cycle goes on uninterrupted, trouble inevitably lies ahead. Jillian's behavior will deteriorate, and home will become a constant battleground.

seven or eight, this pattern may have an additional unfortunate by-product: both parent and child feel mistreated, and their relationship deteriorates. But Cool Down can break such a cycle.

Using the Cool Down technique has two goals. The first is to change the child's initial defiant behavior for which he was reprimanded. The second and more important goal is to end the spiraling angry interchanges that often follow reprimands. When used in precisely the prescribed way, Cool Down discourages the child both from repeating the initial misbehavior, and from continuing to act out following a reprimand. Cool Down actually teaches a child to regulate his anger on his own.

As of the time I am writing these words, I have taught Cool Down to well over a thousand parents. Their children have ranged from mildly disobedient to consistently "oppositional"—that is, children who have fallen into the habit of refusing to follow rules or respond to their parents' instructions.* Most of these parents, whose children do the normal things kids do (i.e., misbehave and then become argumentative when corrected) have learned the technique quickly and been able to employ Cool Down on their own without therapeutic intervention. It has immediately proven to be a highly effective discipline tool.

Most parents find that they are best able to apply the Cool Down technique when they understand the logic behind it. The rationale for each step is based on one of the behavioral principles of discipline outlined in Chapter 4. This grounding in behavioral principles makes Cool Down different from—and generally far more successful than—Time-Out and many of its variations as described in other books and articles.

The Behavioral Principles Underlying Cool Down

Each component of Cool Down is based on behavioral principles. This foundation accounts for why parents consistently succeed with Cool Down even though they may not have done well

---

*I have also successfully adapted this technique for parents whose children have other serious mental and developmental conditions. In most of these cases, the families need a trained therapist to help them successfully apply the technique.

with Time-Out or other attempts to put an end to unwanted behaviors.

The basic structure of the Cool Down technique is as follows: First, the parent interrupts the child in the midst of misbehaving and prevents her from continuing to misbehave by placing her in a designated spot. The parent then completely withdraws his attention from the child. While in the Cool Down spot, the child is also isolated from any other people and sources of stimulation. Finally, the child is permitted to leave Cool Down only when her misbehavior has stopped and she is behaving appropriately.

In behavioral terms, making a child stop whatever she is doing by putting her into Cool Down is actually *punishment*. She gets feedback that her current behavior is unacceptable, and a negative consequence immediately follows it.

The more important behavioral principle at work here, however, is *extinction*. In Cool Down, the parent *completely stops responding to what the child was doing prior to being put in Cool Down and also to the child's behavior throughout her time in Cool Down*. Since a parent's attention is the single most powerful tool in discipline, removing that attention immediately when a child begins to misbehave is an extremely effective means of changing that particular behavior. By using the Cool Down technique, the parent applies extinction both to the initial behavior and to any arguments and anger that follow the reprimand.

Managing misbehavior through extinction contrasts sharply with situations like Jillian and her mother's interaction. In that situation, Jillian's mother reinforced her daughter's defiance and escalating anger by giving her a lot of attention at the moment these were occurring. Thus, she actually promoted the continuation, escalation, and recurrence of Jillian's misbehavior.

The final stage of Cool Down is *negative reinforcement*. When the Cool Down period comes to an end, the child is permitted to leave only when she is behaving appropriately. At this point, releasing her from this negative situation reinforces her most recent behavior. Her good behavior is reinforced by removing the negative condition of Cool Down. The important point to be made here is that in order to achieve the disciplinary benefit of Cool Down, parents must follow through on this final stage. It is imperative for the child to act in an appropriate way before she is permitted to leave Cool Down; otherwise, her misbehavior is once again reinforced.

The seemingly simple Cool Down technique is built on the effective structuring of three fundamental behavioral principles of discipline: punishment, extinction, and negative reinforcement. Given this context, parents can see how a seemingly slight change in applying the technique can make all the difference between its success and its failure—or even, in the worst circumstances, its complete backfire.

I encourage parents not only to use the Cool Down technique exactly as it is outlined in this chapter, but also to pay attention to how they apply each aspect of it in context of the underlying behavioral principles. In doing so, they often gain insight not only into how to use Cool Down, but also into how other discipline habits may be improved.

Cool Down Step-by-Step

Parents who *consistently* apply the Cool Down technique *exactly* as described in this section have a high probability of succeeding with it. The reason for consistency has already been explained— clear, consistent, contingent consequences are fundamental to the success of any discipline technique. The word *exactly* is stressed because the difference between parents' success and failure with this technique often lies in how they administer its details.

This Cool Down technique has been refined and polished to apply punishment, extinction, and finally negative reinforcement at the right moments and in the right context to achieve the desired disciplinary outcome.

1. Choose a Specific Cool Down Location

The goal of picking a spot for Cool Down is to create a physical situation that completely lacks stimulation—in a word, the child must find it *boring*. The proverbial "padded room" would be the ideal Cool Down spot, but—through some accident of American architecture—this is not part of most households!

The point of finding such a location is not to humiliate the child, but to remove him from all stimulation. For this reason, the spot must be chosen so that it prevents the child from encountering anything at all that interests him—people, TV, stereo, radio, games, and so on. The Cool Down spot should be a place where a child can calm down, not by distracting himself with pleasurable things, but by being isolated from virtually everything. A final condition is that the location must be specified in precise terms— a particular chair or a specific stair step.

Applying these conditions means that the family room, TV room, playroom, kitchen, and child's bedroom almost never make effective Cool Down spots. There are two reasons for this. The first is that these rooms almost always contain many means for a child to have fun. When he has access to toys, books, games, people, and other means of stimulation and entertainment, he is not really in Cool Down. The second reason is that once a child becomes accustomed to the Cool Down technique, he often begins to seek solitude voluntarily whenever he feels the need to calm himself. At these times, he usually chooses to go to his own room. Under these circumstances, the bedroom can be an appropriate, comfortable place for the child to settle down. Every child needs a comfortable place that is distinctively his own, so it is important not to turn a bedroom into a punishment spot.

Locations that have proven both practical and effective include a chair turned to face the corner (ideally in a seldomly used room such as a living room or dining room), a specific enclosed stair step, a blank wall at the end of a closed hallway, and a laundry room. Although many parents initially struggle to find a Cool Down spot that is truly isolated—particularly when they have more than one child—they always manage to find one that works. Ideally, the location would have the advantage of being easily translated into many other locations away from home, as well as being completely and desirably boring.

In order to preclude possible arguments, the parent should identify each child's Cool Down spot with a sticker or some other mark. In this way, whether or not a child is in his Cool Down spot at any given time is never open to question.

2. Get a Mechanical Kitchen Timer for Each Child

The purpose of having a timer is for the child to see the amount of time remaining in her Cool Down, and not just the passing of time. A wind-up kitchen timer with a marker that moves as the minutes tick by and a bell that rings at the end usually works perfectly. Although many people have tried using a digital timer, the stove clock, or a wristwatch, none of these allows a young child to understand how many minutes she has left in Cool Down. Even if the child is precocious or already able to subtract, this is not the time to concentrate on the subtraction lesson. It is a time for her to be thoroughly bored and keep watching the very slow movement of the timer to see how many more minutes she must stay in her Cool Down.

Each child in the household must have her own Cool Down timer and be able to identify it clearly. This can be accomplished by buying a timer in a different color for each child, or by marking each one with a child's name in large letters. The reason that each child must have her own is precisely the same as why each child must have her own Marble Jar (see Chapter 5). The timer, like the Marble Jar, takes on its own identity as the discipline tool. In the child's mind (especially after the parent helps to establish the concept), it very quickly becomes the timer, and not the parent, that "tells" a child when she may leave Cool Down. Having her own timer is more important than it may seem on the surface, because this "ownership" helps to reinforce the notion that the child has ultimate responsibility for her own behavior.

3. *Use These Instructions to Place the Child in Cool Down*

1. Give the child the instruction or command in a firm but neutral voice. Do not express anger through your voice, gesture, or facial expression. For example, say, "You are to pick up your toys and put them away now," or "You are to stop screaming right now."

COOL DOWN STEPS

1. Give the command.
2. Within thirty seconds, give a warning.
3. Place the child in Cool Down.
4. Set the timer.
5. Allow the child to leave when the bell rings if the child has behaved well for at least thirty seconds.

---

2. If the child does not comply within thirty seconds (absolutely no longer), say, "This is your warning. If you do not [restate what you have just asked the child to do or stop doing] now, you will go in Cool Down." Use a voice that is even more firm and serious, but do not raise your voice or express anger, and do not add any other words. At this point, parents are sometimes drawn into the trap of responding to a child's questions or pleas for more time. For the behavioral reasons explained in the section "The Behavioral Principles Underlying Cool Down," it is counterproductive to do so.

3. If the child has not begun to comply within thirty seconds, say "Cool Down" in a firm but still not angry tone of voice. Refrain from the temptation to say anything else. From this point forward, do not talk to the child, make eye contact, or in any other way express anger or any other emotion. If it is necessary to physically escort the child to the Cool Down place, do so without comment. Occasionally, a parent at first may have difficulty getting a child to go into the Cool Down spot. Techniques to handle this will be addressed in the next chapter.

4. When the child is seated in the Cool Down spot, set the timer in a place where the child can see it but not reach it. It is very important to explain to the child during the teaching session on Cool Down that he is not to touch the timer. Set it for 10 minutes for a child of four or older. For a two-year-old, use 2 minutes, and for a three-year-old, use 5 minutes. The rationale for these amounts of time is explained below.

5. If the child has been quiet and nondisruptive for at least thirty seconds before the timer goes off, allow him to leave Cool Down when the bell rings. Sometimes after a child becomes accustomed to Cool Down, he may choose to stay in the Cool

Down spot for longer than the assigned time. If this is the case, by all means allow him to do so. He likely is working on managing his own behavior, and he will leave when he feels ready. This is understandable, particularly as the child begins to understand that he can use Cool Down as a means of self-discipline.

4. Do Not Speak to a Child in Cool Down Except in These Two Circumstances

The first is when the child is still not being quiet when the timer goes off. At this point, the parent calmly says to the child, "You were not quiet when the timer went off. You get another five minutes." The parent then resets the timer and walks away without saying anything else. Although it may be tempting to release a child from Cool Down when she is not yet quiet, doing so would—in behavioral terms—reinforce the disruptive misbehavior.

Conversely, it does not matter what the child has been doing during the first nine and a half minutes of Cool Down. If she is quiet for at least thirty seconds immediately before the timer goes off, she should be allowed to leave Cool Down. Thirty seconds is sufficient "good behavior" time; releasing the child at that point will reinforce the good behavior. The disruptive behavior will automatically be extinguished without the parent having to do anything further about it.

The second circumstance in which a parent speaks to a child in Cool Down is when she physically leaves contact with the assigned Cool Down spot. Then the parent says, "You are off the stair (or out of your chair). You get another five minutes." As with the previous situation, the parent is to reset the timer, but not to say anything else and not to express any anger.

The rule should be made so that if even the tiniest part of the child's body is touching the Cool Down spot, she is "in," and if no spot touches, she is "out." This prevents arguments about whether the child is in or out.

5. Explain and Practice the Cool Down Procedure with the Child Before Using It for the First Time

When parents first introduce Cool Down, it is best if both of them can sit down and explain it at a quiet, pleasant time when no one is upset about anything. They begin by setting a positive context—telling the child that they are really happy when he behaves well, and that it is important for him to learn how to be on his best behavior more of the time. They explain that all the family and babysitters will start to use a new way (or a little bit different way, if the family previously has used a version of Time-Out) to help him learn to manage his behavior.

Then they show the child the assigned Cool Down place and talk him through every step that will occur. They explain which behaviors will result in Cool Down, making clear to him the if-then nature of the misbehavior and its consequences. For instance, they may say, "If you disobey one of us after we have asked you to do something, or if you act up—you know, scream or cry, or try to hurt something—then you will be put in Cool Down." They tell him that he is to go there (or for a younger child, be taken there) immediately upon being told to go to Cool Down. Then they explain that the timer will be set for a certain number of minutes, and they tell him how many minutes that will be. He is not to touch the timer and not to come out of Cool Down until the bell rings. He will not be allowed to have any toys or books or talk to anyone. They explain that they will not speak to him while he is in Cool Down, no matter what. Finally, they tell him that if he is still misbehaving before the Cool Down bell rings, more minutes will be set on the timer, and he will have to stay there for the additional time.

If the parents have already been using a different version of Time-Out, they explain to the child that Cool Down is a lot like Time-Out, but now they will start to use the new Cool Down rules. They make sure he understands exactly how Cool Down will operate and answer any of his questions about the new rules versus the old Time-Out rules.

What to Expect

Five steps—five fairly simple steps—are all it takes to use this Cool Down discipline technique effectively. This is not to suggest, however, that a single session in Cool Down will correct a child's misbehavior.

When parents first begin to use this technique, in most cases the child continues to act out after she is placed in Cool Down. After all, she is angry and probably has formed a habit of arguing and displaying her anger. But as long as there is a consistent lack of response to this display, this pattern of behavior soon comes to an end. As new situations arise, the child is less and less likely to respond with heightened anger, knowing that it will not get her any attention.

Even after Cool Down has been in place for some time, most children still break the rules or act out on occasion. But if parents immediately respond by placing the child in Cool Down, most are surprised to find that the need to use it generally diminishes more quickly than they had anticipated.

One reason why Cool Down is so successful is that the parent employs it before a child's behavior goes wildly out of control. Since the parent uses only three commands in a very short period of time, he interrupts the behavior and the reaction before the child's anger has a chance to escalate to a peak level. Thus, the child complies before she reaches the shrieking stage. She may scream once she is in Cool Down, but completely ignoring that behavior will extinguish it automatically. Using Cool Down in the calm, quiet, and absolutely boring way described here thus extinguishes the initial undesirable behavior as well as the arguments and anger that typically follow, and then reinforces the quiet, compliant behavior that occurs before the child is released. With the behavioral principles thoroughly integrated and operational, Cool Down achieves its ends.

What Can Go Wrong: The Most Common Mistakes

Since many parents are accustomed to using Time-Out, and since Cool Down is a variation on this technique, it may be helpful to understand what often goes wrong with Time-Out and why, before trying to adopt Cool Down.

Most of the reasons that cause parents to claim that Time-Out "doesn't work" can be traced to a fundamental problem with the particular way they are using the Time-Out technique. Almost inevitably, some aspects of their technique contradict behavioral principles.

Time-Out was originally designed to provide "time out from positive reinforcement." By far the most common problem I identify when parents describe their frustration with Time-Out is that the *intended withdrawal of positive reinforcement never occurs at all.* As described in Chapter 4, giving any attention at all to a particular behavior serves to reinforce it. So paradoxically, negative attention generally provides an all-too-powerful means of positive reinforcement for an unwanted behavior. The parent sends the child to Time-Out, but then continues to interact with him. The child persists in asking questions, which the parent answers, or the child yells and the parent responds. Sometimes their inter-

FIVE-YEAR-OLD Charlie decided he'd had just about enough of his new brother. He had been gentle with Teddy when he was an infant, but now the ten-month-old was crawling around, drooling and chewing on Charlie's toys, messing up his train set, and taking all too much of Mom's time and attention.

So now when Teddy would come along dragging his brother's toys, Charlie just grabbed the toys or pushed Teddy . . . or both. The minute Teddy started crying, Charlie knew what was coming: Mom would say, "Time-Out."

It made him mad. When Mom put him in Time-Out, he started by calling out, "Why do I have to go into Time-Out?" From the next room, she would explain that he had pushed his brother. Then he'd complain, "It's not fair. You always take his side." Mom would patiently explain, but Charlie would keep on whining. Finally, he would start shouting, and then Mom would get mad. Sometimes she would even come back into his room and yell at him. On and on it went, until Time-Out finally ended, one way or another.

Mom concluded that Time-Out did not work. But when, exactly, did Time-Out occur? The real answer is that it never did, because Mom and Charlie never stopped interacting.

changes even escalate into significant displays of anger on both sides.

In such situations, who is in Time-Out? Certainly not the child! In fact, *this is exactly how a parent mistakenly provides positive reinforcement for the child's misbehavior by continuing to give attention— a lot of attention!—to it.*

The situation that Charlie and his mom find themselves in occurs over and over in many households, with the only changes being the names, the child's age, and the specific behavior that triggered the Time-Out. What do not change are the ongoing interaction between parent and child and its outcomes: persistent misbehavior from the child and frustration from the parent. The example reveals how by continuing to give Charlie her attention, Mom actually reinforces his misbehavior, rather than extinguishing it.

Another extremely common problem is caused by the *flawed notion that the child must calm down before being placed in Time-Out.* Generally, this delay allows for an escalation of the problem behavior and the emotions that accompany it. The child winds up screaming and crying, and the parent, with mounting frustration, follows suit. If and when the child does calm down, the parent then puts her in Time-Out—thus the punishment immediately follows the child's good behavior rather than her misbehavior. In this case, the child's misbehavior is not effectively addressed, while her improved behavior is actually punished.

A third error that commonly occurs in Time-Out involves *following the incorrect formula that assigns one minute of Time-Out for every year of the child's age.* Seen from a behavioral perspective, it is evident that most four-year-olds take far longer than four minutes to achieve calm once they have gotten out of control. And an angry seven-year-old is no more likely to calm down in seven minutes than the four-year-old child is in four minutes. In order for extinction and negative reinforcement to take place—and thus for this discipline technique to achieve its goals—the amount of Time-Out must be assigned based on when the individual child can reasonably be expected to calm down. Since the most important goal of Cool Down is to help the child learn to regulate his anger, sufficient time must be allowed for him to settle down. The amount of time required corresponds to the child's developmental stage, which does not equate to one minute per year of age.

Overall, *inconsistency is another very common problem in the use of Time-Out.* While setting rules and applying them consistently seem easy on the surface, the reality is that parents have plenty on their minds all the time, and interpreting behavior day by day can be more complicated than it sometimes seems.

For instance, parents generally want to teach their children not to throw food on the floor. But sometimes, dumping soup on the dog's head or perfectly landing a strand of spaghetti on the chore chart can be side-splittingly funny, and then discipline goes completely awry. This is not a problem if it is a very rare exception. But if one day a child is sent to Time-Out for a particular misdeed, and the next day she repeats it with no consequences, she becomes confused. In such circumstances, she then generally does whatever pleases herself. Thus, as in all discipline, Time-Out is truly effective only when it is applied clearly and consistently as a contingent consequence, day after day.

One final point: consistency is achieved only when *all* of the child's caregivers agree to use the same discipline techniques in the same way for the same purposes. So Time-Out, Cool Down, and all other discipline techniques are effective only to the degree that mother, father, grandmother, grandfather, and babysitter all agree to insist on the same set of behaviors and to apply discipline in the same, clear, structured way. Without such consistency, the child becomes confused and behavior problems are not solved.

These cautions may help parents to avoid some of the common problems with Time-Out as they initiate Cool Down. The next chapter provides further guidance on some specific questions many parents pose as they contemplate this technique.

8

Cool Down: What If . . . ?

I can't believe Cool Down actually worked—and it
didn't take long at all! He actually seemed intrigued
by the concept when I explained it to him. Then,
once he understood that we were serious, he just
went to his chair without arguing. I'm completely
amazed.

As they get ready to use Cool Down, parents usually have
questions. Generally, these arise from their past experiences
using Time-Out or other discipline techniques. This chapter
addresses the "what if's" and "what do I do when's" that parents
ask most frequently.

What if He Won't Stay in Cool Down?

For many parents who have previously used Time-Out, this question is right at the top of their list of concerns—with good reason. In the past, the child has acted out and refused to stay in
Time-Out. So, they wonder, why should Cool Down be any
different?

Children usually stay in Cool Down because specific aspects of its structure are based in sound behavioral theory:

1. First, *the child is sent to Cool Down before he loses control of his temper and behavior.* This affects not only his willingness to stay in Cool Down, but also the overall effectiveness of the discipline imposed.

The child soon learns that Cool Down will be applied consistently according to the preestablished rules and within a very short period of time—before either he or his parent has a chance to get angry. The parent issues an instruction; if the child fails to comply within thirty seconds, he is given a warning. If he has not begun to comply within another thirty seconds, he is sent to Cool Down. Thus, the total elapsed time between the parent's first instruction and placing the child in Cool Down is just one minute—very seldom long enough for a child to lose control. Cool Down also requires the parent to remain calm but firm, rather than to become angry, and this diminishes the likelihood of a heated exchange.

This atmosphere of calm and control that characterizes Cool Down often contrasts sharply with parents' past experiences using Time-Out. Those who have found the latter technique unsuccessful generally report that they invoked Time-Out only when the child was already angry, and sometimes when the parent was steaming, too. Since children often completely lose control of their behavior when they are upset, they will act out even more when they are suddenly confronted by an angry parent shouting, "That's it! Time-Out!"

2. A second factor that influences the child to stay in Cool Down is that *the child understands clearly what the rules are and how Cool Down will work before it is ever applied.* Before they use it for the first time, the parents quietly and clearly explain to the child how Cool Down will work. That way he knows how he

is expected to behave, how he will be warned if he is misbehaving, what will happen while he is in Cool Down, how long he must stay there, and how he must behave in order to be permitted to leave. When he clearly understands both these expectations and the consequences for not meeting them, the child is more likely to comply than when thrust into a situation that he does not fully understand.

In many cases, as the child puts the pieces of the new technique together in his mind, he actually becomes intrigued with it. Because he understands both the rules and the Cool Down process so clearly, he is more likely to comply. Even when a child is angry, the clear structure of Cool Down helps him to understand exactly what is expected of him, and thus increases the likelihood that he will comply.

3. A third critical factor in the child's willingness to stay in Cool Down is *knowing in advance how much time he must spend in Cool Down.* Many times, parents who use Time-Out do so without setting a specific amount of time the child must stay there and/or without making clear how he must behave in order to be allowed to leave. Under these circumstances, the child has no idea when or why he will be able to leave, so he has no clear framework for changing his behavior.

By contrast, the child who is placed in Cool Down knows exactly how many minutes he will be there. Also, the timer in front of him gives him concrete evidence of exactly how much time he has left. He also knows how he must behave before he is released, and that if he fails to behave properly, he will have to stay for another fixed amount of time. Knowing the amount of time and the conditions for leaving gives the child a sense of certainty and tends to reduce or even prevent his anger.

Even with these factors in place, it is not unusual for a child to test the limits the first time or two he is placed in Cool Down. He very well may get up and leave. If he does, it is important to put the child back in Cool Down and add the prearranged number of minutes. By calmly and firmly carrying out the established Cool Down protocols, the parent lets the child know she is sticking to the plan. Through her action, she clearly demonstrates that the structure remains consistently in place.

Sometimes, a child tests Cool Down purely out of curiosity. At other times, a child—especially a young one—tests it simply because she does not yet understand the whole process the first time it is used.

With three-year-old Emma, it was probably a bit of both. The first time her mother put her in Cool Down, she went obediently to her spot. After about thirty seconds, she got up and left. Her mother brought her back and set the timer for another minute, explaining that she must now stay there an extra minute.

Just thirty seconds later, Emma called out, "I'm all done now," and went off to play. Mother brought her back to her spot again, set the timer for another minute, pointed to the timer, and said, "You may not leave until it rings."

"Ding," sang out Emma, just a minute later, and walked off. Mother brought her back and said simply, "The timer has to ding, Emma, not you."

With each of Emma's departures, Mother became more and more amused, and by the time she "dinged," Mother was convulsed with laughter in the kitchen. Fortunately, she managed to hide her hilarity and remained calm and consistent with Emma.

Apparently, this set of experiments was enough to satiate Emma's curiosity and clarify the process. Thereafter, she followed the Cool Down rules perfectly.

Sometimes during the first or second use of Cool Down, the child will leave the Cool Down spot more than once. When he does so, the parent must continue to return him to Cool Down and add more minutes to the timer. It is not unusual for a child to wind up sitting in his Cool Down spot for twenty-five or thirty minutes. But after attempting to leave once or twice and discovering that more Cool Down minutes are added each time, the child soon learns that the parent will follow through and apply the rules. Then he stops testing the system.

On occasion, a child may continue to leave Cool Down repeatedly during the first several times it is invoked. Especially with a younger child, if the timer reaches some unreasonable amount of time—say forty-five minutes—then the parent should recognize that the situation is out of control and bring this Cool Down session to an end. In such a case, placing the child in his room for an hour may help the child to calm down. Although I do not recommend using a child's bedroom as a Cool Down spot, in rare situations—especially when Cool-Down is first used—the bedroom can serve as a place to calm down. If the parent immediately invokes Cool Down the next time the child misbehaves, and invokes it consistently thereafter, the child will soon learn that the parent means business, and will stay in his Cool Down spot.

Most parents have enough control over their children to get them to comply. On rare occasions, a parent may try the Cool Down system but find that the child is still noncompliant after repeated attempts. In such cases, it may be beneficial to seek the help of a professional psychologist.

What if She Refuses to Go to Cool Down?

Surprisingly, this almost never happens. When parents say, "You will go to Cool Down now," the child almost always complies.

Since the system has been clearly and calmly explained in advance, she has a context for this instruction and understands what will happen.

On occasion, however, a child may refuse to go to Cool Down, especially the first time or two that it is invoked. One way to preclude the child's refusal is for both parents (or the parent and primary child-care provider, in the case of single-parent households) to be present the first time Cool Down is used. When two adults show their solidarity and insist on the child obeying the rules, the child is more likely to understand the seriousness of their expectations and intentions. Having this perception, she is more likely to obey than if she deals with only one parent, particularly if she thinks she can outmaneuver that parent.

With a young child under the age of about seven, the parent may need to take her to the Cool Down spot the first time it is invoked. If necessary, the parent may physically take the child by the hand, lead her to the spot, and see that she is seated. Getting the child to comply solely through a verbal instruction, however, is preferable to using any physical contact. Physical contact often causes children to become more reactive and angry—a condition to be avoided whenever possible.

An older child can often be persuaded to go to Cool Down by starting the timer immediately when she shows resistance and telling her that the amount of time she takes getting to the Cool Down spot will be added to her Cool Down minutes. A child of seven or older can do the arithmetic and understand the if-then logic. If she takes a long time to comply, then she will spend more time in an undesirable situation. Therefore, she is likely to comply more quickly and avoid the unpleasant consequences.

One last resort for getting an older child (over the age of seven) to go to Cool Down is to take away privileges. Since the addition of this punishment usually tends to escalate the situation, it is not a desirable technique. But if necessary, it can be used on an occasion when a child is unusually defiant and unwilling to go to Cool Down. If parents find that they need to invoke this technique or are having unusual difficulty gaining their child's compliance, it may be helpful to reexamine their use of Cool Down, step-by-step, and how they are using it in a system of clear, consistent, contingent consequences.

What if He's Having a Meltdown? Shouldn't I Calm Him Down Before I Put Him in Cool Down?

This is a critical difference between the Cool Down technique and some versions of the Time-Out technique as described in other books. Of course, it is difficult to put a screaming, hysterical child into Cool Down and walk away. No parent finds this easy. But if a child's angry, defiant behavior is to be extinguished, this is exactly what must happen.

Occasionally, a child's hysteria is a product of fear rather than anger. If this is the case, he may need to be comforted. Children have predictable fears at certain developmental stages.

One example of an outburst caused by either fear or anger is an upset at bedtime. If a three-year-old begins to shriek when he is left in a dark room, he may be afraid. If the parents determine that this is the case, it would be appropriate for them to comfort the child and then to change the bedtime situation so that he is not left in a totally dark room. If the same type of bedtime disturbance occurs with a seven-year-old, however, it is likely that he is trying to manipulate his parents. In this situation, it is almost always best for them to put an immediate stop to this behavior.

The fundamental question that parents must answer when their child is out of control is whether the meltdown is the result of anger or whether it is the product of fear. In the vast majority of cases, children's tantrums are caused by anger. In these cases, parents will most effectively discourage repeat tantrums by withdrawing their attention. Should a child be truly anxious and afraid, then the opposite is true, and he probably does need his parents' attention to help him deal with those feelings. In rare cases, an older child may have outbursts because of some irrational fear; in such a situation, the parents may need to seek guidance from a professional who specializes in children's behavior.

One final note about meltdowns and Cool Down: this technique is easiest to apply and most effective if it is enforced immediately, *before* a child's emotions are out of control.

What If She Has to Go to the Bathroom While She Is in Cool Down?

A child who is fully toilet trained and has had no accidents for a long time can control her urges for the ten minutes or so that Cool Down is in effect. So usually, a request to go to the bathroom is a ploy to get attention, and it is best ignored. Anticipating that a child will likely make this request, however—after all, it is a common stalling tactic—parents are well advised to address it when first explaining Cool Down to their child. The parents should explain to her that she may not leave the Cool Down spot to go to the bathroom, get a drink of water, answer the telephone, or anything other than respond to a genuine emergency.

Because Cool Down is an effective technique for younger children who are still being toilet trained or have occasional accidents, however, parents of little ones do sometimes need to deal with potty breaks during Cool Down. With a child of this age, the parent must judge whether the urge is genuine or whether the child is simply trying to get attention. If he decides that the child's need is real, the parent should escort her to the bathroom with as little interaction as possible. When the child is finished, the parent should immediately escort her back to the Cool Down spot and increase the minutes on the timer to account for the time spent going to the bathroom. If the child asks to go to the bathroom a second time during the same Cool Down session, it is almost certainly a ploy to get attention and should be ignored. As with other aspects of the technique, the parent should explain to the child in advance that if she needs to leave Cool Down to go to the bathroom, the time she is away from her spot will be added to her Cool Down minutes.

What If He Hurts Himself While in Cool Down?

In all the years I have used this technique with my clients, I have never known a child to hurt himself during Cool Down. This is not to say that it cannot or will not happen, but it is unlikely to occur.

What a child more likely will do is try to get his parents' attention by appearing to do something harmful or saying he is hurt. The parent must assess such situations. If it is clear that a child is simply acting out to get attention and is in no physical danger, the most effective way for parents to handle the situation is to ignore it, since giving attention to this behavior only reinforces it and encourages the child to repeat it.

If a child has been in the habit of hurting himself during times when he is very angry and his behavior is completely beyond his own control, parents may find that the Cool Down technique helps bring these episodes to an end. With Cool Down, the parent intervenes quickly, before the child's emotions escalate to such a perilous level. Thus, the situation that has perpetuated a harmful habit may be successfully interrupted.

A very few children do repeatedly hurt themselves when they are disciplined. If a child persists in banging his head, biting himself, or doing other genuinely harmful things to himself, then the parents need to seek professional help.

What if Her Brothers and Sisters Will Not Leave Her Alone?

Allowing other children to interact with a child in Cool Down will negate the benefits of this technique. Parents can help ensure the technique's success by establishing a Cool Down spot that is isolated from family activities, and by making and enforcing a family rule that requires siblings to stay away from a child in Cool Down. When parents first start using Cool Down, siblings are likely to be curious about it, and they are more likely to interfere at this point than after the novelty wears off. It is important for parents to put time, thought, and effort into setting up the Cool Down system so that it is effective from the outset.

For families who are likely to use Cool Down with more than one child simultaneously, it is important to establish a separate spot for each child. Each should be out of the path of family activity and away from other siblings' Cool Down spots. Because houses are not always built with multiple boring corners in convenient locations away from family activities, parents may need to be inventive in establishing these spaces.

In fact, they may need to create them by removing other children from the Cool Down environment, rather than building new nooks into the house! At times, especially early in the use of this technique, parents may simply need to herd other children into a place where it is impossible for them to talk to, tease, or even look at the child in Cool Down. Distracting siblings with other activities—even putting them in front of the TV—may help to establish the pattern of Cool Down isolation early on, while this technique is still tenuous. Once the technique is established and familiar, siblings usually pay less attention, so the parents may not need to take extraordinary measures to keep other siblings separate from the Cooling Down child.

If parents plan to use this technique to deal with fighting between siblings, particularly if aggression is involved, they will need to invoke simultaneous Cool Downs. Since these circumstances require parents to take charge of two or more children at once, it is helpful for both parents to be on hand when they first use the technique. After it is established and understood, one parent can use it on her own.

What if He Acts Up Someplace Away from Home?

One of the great benefits of Cool Down is that it is "portable" and can be administered almost anywhere. In fact, by using Cool Down consistently at home and away from home, parents show children that they expect them to behave by the same rules and standards all the time and everywhere.

One way parents can foster good behavior away from home is to make clear to the child that they will use Cool Down away from home. When explaining Cool Down the very first time, parents should tell the child that they can and will use the technique anywhere they go. Then they reinforce this understanding by positively reminding the child each time they leave the house that they fully expect him to be on his best behavior at their destination, and that the same rules apply there as do at home. They also tell him they are taking the Cool Down timer along, just in case it's needed. Then they follow through and pack the Cool Down timers anytime they leave the house with their children. These are, after all, the obvious symbols of the consequence of misbehaving, and simply taking them along makes a powerful statement. Soon parents will not need to talk about expectations every time they step out the door; packing the timers will be a sufficient reminder.

At Someone's Home

In using Cool Down at someone else's home, a parent should take a few quiet minutes with the child soon after arrival and select a place that will be the Cool Down spot, if it is needed. This is a good time for the parent to tell him that she really believes that he will behave well because he understands the rules, and the rules are the same here as they are at home.

If the child misbehaves, it is important for the parent to follow through and use Cool Down. If the parent feels uncomfortable about making a scene, she may take comfort in remembering that applying this technique now will help prevent the need for it in the future.

In a Public Place

When a child misbehaves in a public place, the parent has two choices regarding discipline.

The first choice, and the more powerful of the two, is to take immediate action. If the parent has a car nearby, she can immediately take the child there and place him in a car seat or the backseat. If it is hot, of course, she rolls down the windows. The parent then stands outside the car, leaning with her back against the door so that the child can see her, but she does not look at the child. She holds the timer in her hand so that the child can see it

DOMINIC LEARNED A lesson on one memorable trip to the grocery store. He was cranky and whined repeatedly. His mother ignored him. Trying to get her attention, he began screaming. His mother told him, "Dominic, you know you are not to scream. If you scream again, you will go in Cool Down." Now Dominic was no dummy. He was sitting in a fairly full grocery cart, and his mother was still searching for items on her list. So he decided it was safe to scream again.

He was shocked when his mother said, "That's it, Dominic—Cool Down." In a flash, she wheeled the cart to the service counter and told the clerk, "Please hold onto this for me, I'm coming back." Then she lifted Dominic from his seat and carried him off to the car, where she invoked Cool Down. Once it was finished, she and Dominic went back to the store, retrieved the cart, and finished shopping . . . quietly.

Dominic discovered that his mother meant business. That was the last time he acted up in the grocery store.

through the window, and then follows the standard Cool Down procedure. In order to use the car as a Cool Down spot, the parent must be confident that the child will not play with the cigarette lighter, put the car in gear, or otherwise put himself or anyone else in danger.

Often, a parent may be in a situation that makes it difficult to leave immediately. If she is in the midst of grocery shopping, for instance, it is very inconvenient to leave a partially filled cart in the store and walk out with an unruly child. Chances are, however, that the child realizes this and is using the situation to his advantage. If the parent invokes an immediate Cool Down in a public place, the child is often so shocked that he seldom, if ever, misbehaves in such a place again. In situations such as grocery shopping, of course, the parent can return to the store and finish her task after the Cool Down.

The second option is to invoke a delayed Cool Down, to be administered immediately upon returning home. In this situation, the parent tells the child that his behavior is unacceptable, and that he will go into Cool Down as soon as they get home. Ideally, the parent then minimizes interaction with the child from the moment of his misbehavior through the trip home. The parent follows through and places the child in Cool Down the instant they walk through the door, using the normal procedures. At this point, she reminds him why he is being put into Cool Down and then stops interacting with him.

This delayed Cool Down is generally less effective than an immediate action. If, however, the parent has been administering Cool Down consistently, and the child feels very certain that he will go into Cool Down as soon as he gets home, he may decide to correct his behavior immediately.

The delayed Cool Down is more effective with children over the age of five than it is with younger children. By the time they get home, little ones often cannot remember what they did wrong, whereas older children can connect the Cool Down consequence to their misdeed.

Can I Use Cool Down for Aggressive Acts?

Cool Down can be a highly effective discipline technique for children who use physical aggression, but the parents must make one modification. When a child hits, kicks, bites, pinches, or in any way tries to deliberately hurt someone else, she must go into Cool Down immediately, with no warning.

When siblings fight, they often come running to a parent, complaining about each other and "who started it." Frequently, the parent does not know who did what. In this situation, the most effective approach is for the parent to refuse to listen to their accusations. Instead, he calmly tells the children, "You have two choices. You can work this out between yourselves without fighting, or you will both go to Cool Down." By acting on this warning, he discourages them both from fighting and from tattling in the future.

If a parent knows how a fight began or how the children behaved toward each other during a fracas, he will be most successful if he addresses it immediately and directly. By saying, "I know what happened, and here's what we are going to do about it," he takes charge of the situation and administers discipline that can reduce the likelihood of recurrences. By contrast, if he asks a child for a confession or an explanation when he already knows what happened, he not only delays the consequence, but also puts the child in the situation of deciding whether to tell the truth or to lie—not a habit to be encouraged.

What if My Spouse (or Other Caregiver) Refuses to Use Cool Down?

Parents will far more effectively terminate a child's undesirable behaviors if *both* parents use the same technique in the same way for the same set of agreed-upon behaviors. When one parent uses Cool Down and the other does not, the child experiences inconsistency. The same is true if other primary caregivers—grandparents, day-care providers, babysitters, or others who are responsible for the child on a daily basis—use different rules or methods. These discrepancies can confuse a young child (under the age of five or six), leaving him uncertain about how to behave and less likely to change those behaviors that the parent sees as undesirable.

If one parent is committed to using Cool Down, she will benefit the child if she can persuade the spouse or other caregiver to agree to it. A starting point for this discussion is to agree that one or more of the child's behaviors needs to change, and that they both need to help him make the desired changes.

If they can agree on those critical matters, then they may agree to use a single set of rules and to apply the same technique to change their child's behavior. Both caregivers can gain a common understanding of the Cool Down technique by reading this book, or at least Chapters 6 and 7. Then they can talk through and agree upon exactly how they will structure and use Cool Down, and for what specific purposes.

Children who go to day care, preschool, or even the first years of elementary school are usually in an environment where a system of discipline is in place. The rules in this environment may differ slightly from those at home, and the methods of discipline may differ as well. In these situations, it is important to help the child understand that even though there are different rules at home and at school, he must comply with the rules in both places.

It may also help to talk with the day-care provider or teacher, particularly when a child is having difficulty at home or at school. By sharing information about what the child is doing and what each responsible adult is doing about the child's misbehavior, they can better reinforce each other's discipline.

What Do I Say When . . . ?

Everybody has an opinion on child discipline, or so it sometimes seems. Well-intentioned (and sometimes not-so-well-intentioned) relatives, friends, and even strangers offer comments or advice. When using Cool Down, parents may find it helps to have a few responses ready.

When in Someone Else's Home

Sometimes host relatives or friends object when a parent invokes Cool Down. A parent can respond by simply telling them that he is using a technique to help his child learn to behave well all the time, that consistency is important, and that he would appreciate their support.

When the Neighbors Comment

Chances are, if the neighbors are within earshot, they already know when their neighbor child misbehaves. If they comment, it may make parents feel better to say, "I'm learning some new techniques for dealing with my child's behavior." Then let it go at that. After all, the neighbor is not raising the child.

When Standing Against the Car Door Holding a Timer in a Busy Parking Lot

Since this is an unusual sight, sometimes strangers will make comments. When this happens, I suggest that the parent look the person straight in the eye and say, "A psychologist told me to do this." The stranger may decide that the psychologist is crazy, but passing the buck may help the parent feel a little less self-conscious.

In General

Whatever pressures parents feel, they need to remain focused on and confident in the system of discipline they are applying.

After all, one of their primary responsibilities as parents is to help their children learn how to behave appropriately. Consistency is critical to success. Cool Down and the other techniques described will yield results, and the payback will come soon, when the child behaves well at home and away from home and thereby earns the admiring glances and praise of relatives, friends, and strangers. Effective discipline soon proves its worth. The better behaved the child, the more she avoids negative consequences like Cool Down, and the more she is reinforced by praise for her good behavior. Externally imposed discipline thus turns into self-discipline.

How Soon Will Cool Down Start to Work?

Parents who use the Cool Down directions supplied in Chapter 7 frequently report dramatic improvement within one or two weeks after they first implement it. The first signal that Cool Down is working is when a child responds by changing his behavior when he is given the Cool Down warning. This indicates that he understands the consequence of his behavior, remembers what it is like to be in Cool Down, and decides to stop the behavior rather than risk going into Cool Down. Most parents find that after a few weeks, they may need to continue using the warning from time to time, but they seldom need to put the child in Cool Down.

Cool Down may be reinstituted if an undesirable behavior resurfaces, or if a child begins to engage in a new behavior that parents want to stop. In these situations, the parents need to agree on how they will use Cool Down and tell the child that the defined behavior will result in Cool Down. In most cases, they will not need to explain Cool Down again to the child—he will remember!

Some Tips for Success

Learning Cool Down, especially if parents and children are learning it to replace either another Time-Out technique or other old habits, often means making some small but significant changes in individual or family habits. The following factors can help influence the success of Cool Down from the outset:

1. Explain Cool Down thoroughly to the child before using it the first time. Actually show her the timer and walk her to the Cool Down spot. Make sure she understands what she may and may not do while she is in Cool Down. If the parents have been using a Time-Out technique, they should explain how this new technique differs from what they have done before.

2. Try to use Cool Down for the first time on a weekend or at another time when both parents are available and not pressed for time. This allows them to clarify how it works and insist on the child's compliance.

3. Ensure that the elapsed times between the initial instruction and the warning, and between the warning and the Cool Down are very brief. Making these time frames short will help to keep the situation calm and prevent either children or parents from having tempers flare out of control.

4. Remember that one critical aspect of Cool Down is to remove the parents' attention from the child. Do not add any unnecessary words to instructions, and refrain from the impulse to answer anything the child says, no matter how provocative.

5. Remain calm. Particularly if a parent and child have become embattled in the past, the child is very familiar with how to trigger the parent's anger. The very act of staying calm signifies an

entirely different type of discipline, and is far more likely to result in the desired change in the child's behavior.

6. If all else fails, reread the previous chapters, and compare the principles of the 4 Cs and the Cool Down instructions to the system actually put into place. Chances are, there is a flaw in the system that can be detected and corrected.

Although parents may worry about many "what ifs" before they begin using Cool Down, and they are certain to confront some hurdles such as critical grandparents, other active children, and inconvenient places, parents will probably be surprised to find how easy this technique is to learn and to use. Best of all, they'll find how effective it is.

9

Putting It All Together: Achieving the Final "C"

> The atmosphere in our house has really changed.
> Now it seldom feels like a battleground—or
> even a minefield—whereas we used to tiptoe our
> way around imminent explosions. It's a little
> embarrassing to admit it, but I'd forgotten how
> much I like my family!

Shortly after they begin to apply Cool Down, No Reply, Praise for the Expected, and the Learned Rewards System, most parents discover not only that their children are better behaved, but also that the atmosphere in their home has changed. Their reward for using the 4 Cs—clear, consistent, contingent consequences—is a fifth C: calm!

Sometimes it takes a few weeks for calm to emerge. This is largely because it takes children a little time to absorb the new patterns of discipline. Once children realize that their parents are applying the same contingent consequences day after day, however, their behavior begins to improve. With more consistent discipline, children can better predict the consequences of their behavior. With this knowledge, they can improve their ability to

1

manage both their behavior and their emotions. The cumulative effect of the changes in parents' and children's behavior is that the household environment takes on a whole new quality. The home feels like it is emotionally "in order." Especially in families previously torn apart by discord and anger, the difference can be dramatic and healing.

As parents begin to use the new techniques outlined in this book, they often need to revisit some fundamental questions. Then they can set up a system of discipline that consistently encourages good behavior and discourages misbehavior. By analyzing their own families in the context of two essential questions, parents generally can develop a structure that works for their particular situation. The basic questions are

1. Which behaviors do you want your children to change, and how can you accomplish that?
2. How does your own behavior influence your children's?

Which Behaviors Do You Want Your Children to Change?

Using the techniques outlined in this book, parents can influence their children's learned behaviors—that is, behaviors over which the children have some control. These include positive behaviors such as performing chores, taking on independent responsibilities, completing tasks on time, and behaving pleasantly and cooperatively. Learned behaviors also include undesirable behaviors such as aggression, defiance, and a variety of unpleasant behaviors called "bad manners."

Discipline reinforces desirable behaviors and extinguishes undesirable ones.

The fundamental purpose of discipline is to *reinforce the desirable* behaviors and *extinguish the undesirable* ones. Tables 9.1 and 9.2 provide quick references that parents can use as they consider which behaviors they want their children to change and which techniques they can use to impact these behaviors. In addition, parents may want to refer to the developmental chart in the Appendix to clarify whether their children are developmentally ready to take on various kinds of responsibilities and to control certain types of behavior.

How Does Your Own Behavior Influence Your Children's?

Many parents find it relatively easy to analyze which of their children's behaviors they want to change. With some careful thought and planning, they can usually arrive at a discipline strategy that encourages positive behaviors and discourages negative ones. What parents find more difficult is to realize how they themselves influence their children's behavior. Most of us have a few habits so ingrained that we are not even aware of how they impact others. When those "others" are children, the impact may be more powerful than we realize.

When do you give your children the most attention? When do you give them the least? Giving and withdrawing your own attention are the most powerful consequences of all.

The essential questions for parents to ask in assessing their own behavior are these: *When and why do you give your children the most attention? When and why do you give them the least?* Table 9.3 lists

Table 9.1 Behaviors to Encourage

Behaviors	Examples	Discipline Techniques
Chores	Put away toys Set table Wash dishes Do household cleaning tasks	Learned Rewards
Independence Responsibility	Get dressed without help Get ready for bed on own Pick up after self	Learned Rewards
Timeliness	Get ready for school by a predetermined time Get ready for bed on time Finish homework on time	Learned Rewards

Cooperative
Compliance
	Perform chores or
	  responsibilities without
	  being reminded
	Do assigned tasks
	  without complaint
	Agree or offer to help
		Praise for the
		Expected

some common ways in which parents give or fail to give attention to their children. In each case, the outcome (in behavioral terms) is the opposite of what parents generally intend. In the best case, the parents miss opportunities to influence their children to behave better. In the worst, the parents actually encourage their children to continue and repeat undesirable behaviors.

Table 9.3 presents only a few of the typical situations a parent may encounter. Reading this table, parents can easily see how giving attention actually has an effect opposite to the desired one. In

Table 9.2 Behaviors to Eliminate

Behaviors	Examples	Discipline Techniques
Aggression (should not be tolerated)	Hit, kick, or try to hurt another person or a pet Deliberately damage property Act out in ways that could result in harm	Cool Down—immediate and with no warning
Defiance, uncooperativeness	Refuse to comply with parents' or caregivers' instructions Ignore instructions Refuse to respond to instructions or requests	Cool Down—with warning
Whining, wheedling	Beg for treats Complain Whine or act unpleasant	No Reply

life, however, . . . well, that's another matter altogether! In attempting to analyze the whole discipline picture, parents may find it helpful to focus particularly on their children's negative behaviors and consider their own responses to these. If parents realize that they are giving their children a lot of attention for misbehavior, then they can develop a strategy to change these patterns.

By reflecting on each day's discipline encounters at a quiet time, most parents can view their own behavior fairly objectively. When they analyze their interactions, they can see how giving or withdrawing their own attention has influenced their child's behavior. With this understanding, they have a starting point for creating a more deliberate plan of action.

Table 9.3 The Impact of Giving Attention Ineffectively

Child's Behavior	Parent's Attention	Behavioral Outcome and Impact on Discipline
Fails to comply with instruction	Repeats instruction over and over again; nags	Reinforces noncompliance
Does not perform assigned task (such as getting dressed)	Gives child help doing task or does it for him	Reinforces dependence on parent's help
Defiantly refuses to do as told	Gets angry; yells	Reinforces defiance
Acts up	Discusses misbehavior at length with child	Reinforces misbehavior
Talks during Cool Down	Responds to child while in Cool Down	Fails to extinguish misbehavior
Misbehaves and gets angry	Engages in angry confrontation, then gives up	Reinforces angry behavior, then removes consistent expectation
Behaves desirably in a situation where he often has misbehaved	Ignores child, since he is doing nothing wrong	Fails to reinforce desirable behavior

Making a Plan to Suit Your Children and Family

It may seem odd to actually make a plan for changing children's behavior, but without a deliberate and consistent strategy, force of habit will likely prevail. And who among us would leave our most precious task—raising children to be responsible, productive adults—to happenstance?

The questions in this chapter are to help parents focus on which of their children's behaviors they want to encourage and discourage, and to assess how their own current behavior may influence those. Once parents have answered these questions, I recommend that they create their discipline plan in two stages.

1. First build a base of positive behaviors.
2. Then reduce the repetition of undesirable ones.

The first stage is to build a base of positive behaviors. Most children do many things over the course of the day that fall into the category of "good behavior." Parents often can see opportunities to make some of these positive behaviors more consistent, and a very effective strategy for doing so is to apply Praise for the Expected. If parents need to encourage a child to take more responsibility or do certain tasks better and more consistently, then they may add the Learned Rewards System. Most parents find they can use the Marble Jar on an intermittent basis, since children often will establish and maintain desirable habits for long periods of time.

Once having established this base of desirable behavior and positive reinforcement, parents frequently find that the negative behaviors diminish. Of course, sometimes these negative behaviors don't go away; then parents must determine the best ways to reduce them. No Reply is often a more powerful and effective tool than parents expect it to be, especially if they make very clear to the child that he will be ignored when he behaves in specified undesirable ways. For those times when a child acts out, however, Cool Down generally takes care of the problem quickly.

Kids Grow, Life Changes

Having invested time and energy in analyzing the situation and making their discipline plans, parents must deal with constant change. The good news is that much of this change occurs because their discipline plans and techniques take effect. Life becomes smoother, and longer periods of calm evolve. Then, of course, something changes, and they must reassess the situation and make a new plan. All of this is complicated by having more than one child, more than one parent (of course, no two agree completely!), other family members who have opinions of their own, caregivers outside the family, teachers, new schools, moves, and other curves that life produces.

Most parents tell me that as they gain a better understanding of how their own behavior influences their children, changes occur. Sometimes these are quite remarkable. Even when parents are not conscious of making a plan to bring about change, they usually are more thoughtful and deliberate about discipline. They examine their children's behavior and their own more regularly and more clearly, talk about it, and actively decide what to do. Just by going through this process, parents change the way they think and act, and as a result, they influence their children's behavior.

As I said at the beginning of this book, I have spent my entire professional career working with parents and children. They have been, and continue to be, patient learners, excellent teachers, and all in all, the most remarkable source of inspiration. In my clinical practice, I see hundreds of families each year. Sometimes they come with incredibly difficult problems—more than seems fair for life to hand out. Yet I am constantly uplifted by the amount of love and caring I see parents give, and by the remarkable people who grow from squalling infants into fine adults. These people— these families—are treasures. I just know that your family is one of them.

My very best wishes to you as you continue to polish and cherish every facet of your life with your children.

Appendix: How Basic Developmental Abilities at Each Age Impact Discipline Choices

Developmental Abilities and Limitations	Impact on Discipline	Responsibilities Appropriate to Age
Age 2		
Child cannot think logically yet. Child cannot always predict outcomes of own behavior.	Remove objects not to be touched; take away forbidden objects with a gentle but firm "no."	Child cannot assume responsibility yet.
Language is just beginning to develop. Internal language (thinking) cannot be more advanced than spoken language.	Divert attention when toddler begins to do something you don't want her to do.	Begin encouraging child to cooperate with requests. Encourage toddler to help with dressing, bathing, and feeding.
Ability to use language is necessary to encourage toddler's learning to child's making decisions and controlling his behavior.	Patiently repeat rules over and over, to encourage toddler's learning them.	Ask for help with simple tasks, such as bringing a clean diaper, picking up toys, turning off light switch, and closing drawers. Toddlers like to help doing such simple things.
Child has minimal ability to control impulses, even when told "no."	Whenever possible, ignore undesirable behaviors such as whining or tantrums.	
Child can learn not to do certain things, but only when those behaviors are strongly associated with negative outcomes, such as punishment.	Save loud, negative responses for potentially dangerous situations (running into the street, touching the stove), and thereby help toddler learn to associate a firm, loud "no" with a dangerous activity.	
Child begins to develop autonomy and demonstrate desire for control over certain aspects of her life—hence her favorite sayings: "No!" and "I do it!"	When possible, allow toddler to choose between options to satisfy his desire for control. (Example: Do you want juice or milk?)	

Developmental Abilities and Limitations	Impact on Discipline	Responsibilities Appropriate to Age
Age 3		
Child gains more language skills than a 2-year-old, but still cannot think logically.	Continue to keep objects out of reach and distract child rather than put temptation in her path and then reprimand her.	Continue to encourage cooperation with requests.
Child can remember simple rules, but still often gives in to his impulses.	Continue to remove dangerous objects and to stop dangerous situations immediately and firmly.	Request help with simple errands around the house: ask the child to bring objects to you, relay brief messages to others (e.g., "Tell Daddy it's time for dinner now.").
Child has more fears than at any other age, primarily because logic is only partially developed. (Example: "If water can go down the drain, so can I.")	Repeat simple rules over and over; have 3-year-old repeat them after you.	Assign some simple chores: brush teeth, pick up toys, and help set the table. Usually, just doing these is reinforcement enough, but they can be reinforced with Marble Jar, if needed.
Child learns by repetition. This is why she loves to see the same video and hear the same story over and over; it is also why TV shows repeat same songs and routines.	Begin to use a simplified Cool Down technique: when child is naughty or aggressive, remove him from the situation and place him on a chair or stair step for a few minutes; if he will not stay by himself, hold him there without talking or making eye contact; repeat as necessary. Child may or may not be able to understand timer at this age.	
Child has strong need to exert will, although some of the 2-year-old-type struggles for control begin to subside.		

Developmental Abilities and Limitations	Impact on Discipline	Responsibilities Appropriate to Age
Age 3 (continued)	Avoid power struggles. Be consistent: when you say no, stick to it and ignore her negative response. Do not comfort child when he is angry or distraught over discipline (extinguish these behaviors), but offer plenty of comfort (reinforce) *after* he has calmed down. Soothe fears quickly and efficiently; avoid known fears if possible; remember that paying too much attention to fears only strengthens them. If child seems ready, use Marble Jar to reinforce specific responsibilities and introduce the idea of "earning" computer game or TV time. If she is not ready, wait a few months and try again.	

Developmental Abilities and Limitations	Impact on Discipline	Responsibilities Appropriate to Age
Ages 4–5		
Thinking skills improve from age 3. Child can better understand and remember rules.	Repeat rules often; go over rules before starting a new activity or going on an outing.	Marble Jar activities can include
		• making bed
Until about age 4½, child still cannot think logically; by about age 5½, more logical thinking begins to appear and develops rapidly over next 6 months.	Consistently and lavishly praise expected and desired behaviors. Use the Marble Jar: children can now understand trading marbles for desired activities.	• setting or clearing the table
		• putting away toys
		• putting away clean clothes
		• emptying wastebaskets
		Also use marbles to
Better developed language enables child to improve control over impulses. More effective use of language translates to fewer tantrums.	Do not use logic to explain something when the child is upset; when she is calm, explain simply. Limit discussion of any subject to a few minutes; more will be unproductive.	• encourage greater independence in getting dressed, performing hygiene, and preparing for bed
		• reinforce timely completion of tasks (e.g., use a timer and award a marble for getting dressed in 10 minutes)
Child begins to feel empathy. This allows him to influence some control over aggressive urges, but some children still strike out physically when they don't get their way. The urge to hit diminishes by age 6.	Use a timer (a different one from the Cool Down timer) to help the child understand time limits (e.g., getting dressed for school or reading stories before bed).	• establish nighttime habits (e.g., going to bed on time or staying in bed all night can be traded for morning activities)
Child can use if-then thinking to predict outcome of a behavior (e.g., she chooses not to do certain things	Use a timer to encourage solitary play (e.g., "If you play by yourself for 15 minutes, then I will play with you for 15 minutes.").	

Developmental Abilities and Limitations	Impact on Discipline	Responsibilities Appropriate to Age
Ages 4–5 (continued)		
"because Mommy gets mad if I do"; she also understands that doing certain things earns parents' positive attention.	Use child's developing logic to help him understand sequencing of daily tasks (e.g., break tasks like getting dressed and preparing for bed into small steps, which are performed in a particular order).	
With improved knowledge of numbers, the child begins to understand time and can apply time limits.	Use No Reply to extinguish a behavior; tell the child ahead of time that you will ignore her whenever she behaves a certain way.	
	Use entire Cool Down technique (10 minutes). Immediately address aggressive behaviors. Take timer along whenever leaving home. If you cannot employ Cool Down elsewhere, use it immediately upon return.	
	Do not rationalize unacceptable behavior (e.g., do not excuse rudeness on the basis of the child being tired or hungry). This gives the child permission to behave badly at such times.	

Developmental Abilities and Limitations	Impact on Discipline	Responsibilities Appropriate to Age
Ages 6–7		
Child can use logic well, but also thinks in absolute terms with a strong sense of right and wrong. As a result, she is very insistent about rules and very focused on fairness. ("That's not fair!" is a typical expression.)	Rules rule the day: write them down, and use lists as reminders for the child.	Children now can perform many household chores, including all of the ones previously noted for 4- to 5-year-olds plus tasks such as
Child can tolerate frustration better now than when younger.	Have child use his own watch to help him accomplish tasks on time; time limits are still very useful.	• putting away belongings after school
Child can inhibit impulses most of the time....	At this age, child deserves to hold her own opinions, but not necessarily to set the rules. Determine when you are willing to change rules or	• emptying the dishwasher • dusting and light vacuuming • helping to carry and put away groceries
But child can also plan misbehavior with foresight and logic, and justify misdeeds. ("There's no rule against that!")	decisions and when you are not. Make clear to child when decisions cannot be changed and refuse to get drawn into debate. When you are willing to	If child has difficulty focusing on homework, use a timer and specify a time segment during which the child must concentrate. (Set an amount of
Child loves to argue about anything and becomes strongly attached to her own point of view. She often argues her logic is "right" and others' is "wrong."	consider change, then listen to child's perspective and allow her to negotiate.	time you know he *can* concentrate.) Then reinforce concentration with a marble.
Child can use if-then thinking all the time; he can easily predict outcomes, both good and bad.	Use reasoning when everyone is calm, but have discussions with child only as long as he is still engaged. When he starts to tune out, end the discussion promptly.	

Developmental Abilities and Limitations	Impact on Discipline	Responsibilities Appropriate to Age
Ages 6–7 (continued)		
Child understands time, time limits, and sequencing (e.g., she can understand the rule of doing chores before play). Empathy is usually well developed. Child can now regulate his own behavior based on his ability to predict how it will make others feel. Child cannot think in abstract terms; thus she has difficulty reflecting on her own behavior (e.g., the child often cannot understand or explain *why* she did something wrong).	If Marble Jar has not been introduced earlier, start using it now. Make expectations very clear from the outset, and do not negotiate about the rules for Learned Rewards. Use No Reply or other ignoring tactics only when you plan and explain them ahead of time. Child should clearly understand exactly what behavior will be ignored. For most children at this age, Cool Down is used only occasionally. Now, instead of using it to help child control anger, use it to stop arguments and child's insistence on her own point of view. If Cool Down has been used earlier, parents can now use child's bedroom as a place to settle down. If introducing Cool Down for the first time, follow procedure exactly as described.	

Developmental Abilities and Limitations	Impact on Discipline	Responsibilities Appropriate to Age
Ages 8–9		
With growth in his ability to reason, child develops greater flexibility. At age 8, his thinking is still dominated by the logical and the concrete, but as he approaches age 10, some evidence of abstract thinking may begin to appear.	Parents can almost always successfully use reasoning with child at this stage. Explicitly teach verbal if-then thinking: have child use reason to predict outcomes from various behaviors.	At this stage, child should focus on completing tasks independently. These include chores, homework, and daily living skills. One skill that can be developed further at this stage is food preparation. Child can often fix her own breakfast or simple lunch, and she also can help with more complex kitchen processes.
Toward the end of this age range, child can better reflect on her own behavior; she can better remember why she did something, how she felt, and what she was thinking at the time.	Avoid letting a logical exchange of ideas turn into argument for its own sake. In general, positive reinforcement works well with child at this stage. Introduce or return to the Marble	
At this stage, child is usually very social. He generally turns outward from the nuclear family; often, being with friends is all-important.	Jar if child is having difficulty remembering to do something consistently or if he rarely does some chore the correct way. At this age,	
Arguments over rules can still persist but will diminish if child learns that arguing will not result in her getting her own way.	rewards can include special play dates with friends, as well as TV and computer games.	

Developmental Abilities and Limitations	Impact on Discipline	Responsibilities Appropriate to Age

Ages 8–9 (continued)

Developmental Abilities and Limitations	Impact on Discipline	Responsibilities Appropriate to Age
By this age, child can talk about angry feelings, rather than to allow them to rage out of control. Note: If child cannot control her anger—particularly if she lashes out at others or damages property—and does not respond to the techniques described in this book—it may be appropriate to seek professional help. It is important to address serious behavior problems before child reaches preteen years.	Marbles can serve as token rewards, and allowances can now be introduced as rewards for performing weekly chores. No Reply and other forms of ignoring unwanted behaviors can be used, but are usually less effective at this age than at earlier stages. Now, child may interpret ignoring a behavior as tacit approval of it. In general, punishment should be needed less frequently at this stage. Cool Down can still be a useful technique with some children. By age 9 or 10, however, a child may respond better to being sent to her bedroom, rather than to an isolated Cool Down location. In her own quiet space, she can now use reason to reflect on what has gone wrong and then discuss it rationally when she comes out.	

Developmental Abilities and Limitations	Impact on Discipline	Responsibilities Appropriate to Age
Age 10–Preteen*		
By now the child has developed most of the "equipment" necessary to reason and make decisions.	Continue to communicate clear expectations and hold preteen accountable, even as he assumes more control over his life.	Perform as well as possible in school. Behave according to family, school, and societal rules. Follow through on responsibilities. Treat others with respect and courtesy.
She is still missing, however, a depth of experience in using these skills in sophisticated ways and knowledge of the world. Thus, she still needs guidance and help in making decisions. She also needs rules and discipline to help her remain safe and to further develop her abilities and responsibilities.	Require preteen to earn her pleasure time (e.g., require her to complete specific chores or tasks before playing computer games, watching TV, using the Internet, or talking on the phone).	
The influx of hormones may make emotions and behavior somewhat erratic. The preteen sometimes has uncontrolled bouts of crying, quick flares of anger, fits of wild giggling, sexual urges, and other feelings not entirely under his emotional control. While these have a physiological basis, they are still subject to regulation, and the preteen needs to learn how to manage his emotions even at times when he finds it difficult to do so.	Instead of using Cool Down as a punishment, parents can suggest that the preteen may get control over his emotions by taking time away from the rest of the family. Rewards and punishments that are distant in time or more cumulative (and less immediate) can be used, since the preteen has the ability to place these in a context.	

* At this stage, the specific parenting techniques outlined in this book are usually no longer appropriate. The fundamental concepts on which they are based are still operational, however. Clear, consistent, contingent consequences remain a fundamental basis on which preteens can learn to regulate their behavior. Positive and negative reinforcement, extinction, and punishment still influence how they behave, and parents' attention remains a powerful consequence.

Index